Bootstrap
Leadership

Bootstrap Leadership

to break out, take charge, and move up

STEVE ARNESON

BK

Berrett–Koehler Publishers, Inc.
San Francisco
a BK Business book

Berrett-Koehler Publishers, Inc.
235 Montgomery Street, Suite 650
San Francisco, CA 94104-2916
Tel: (415) 288-0260   Fax: (415) 362-2512   www.bkconnection.com

Ordering Information
Quantity sales. Special discounts are available on quantity purchases by corporations, associations, and others. For details, contact the "Special Sales Department" at the Berrett-Koehler address above.
Individual sales. Berrett-Koehler publications are available through most bookstores. They can also be ordered directly from Berrett-Koehler: Tel: (800) 929-2929; Fax: (802) 864-7626; www .bkconnection.com
Orders for college textbook/course adoption use. Please contact Berrett-Koehler: Tel: (800) 929-2929; Fax: (802) 864-7626.
Orders by U.S. trade bookstores and wholesalers. Please contact Ingram Publisher Services: Tel: (800) 509-4887; Fax: (800) 838-1149; E-mail: customer.service@ingrampublisher services.com; or visit www.ingrampublisherservices.com/Ordering for details about electronic ordering.

Berrett-Koehler and the BK logo are registered trademarks of Berrett-Koehler Publishers, Inc.

Printed in the United States of America

Berrett-Koehler books are printed on long-lasting acid-free paper. When it is available, we choose paper that has been manufactured by environmentally responsible processes. These may include using trees grown in sustainable forests, incorporating recycled paper, minimizing chlorine in bleaching, or recycling the energy produced at the paper mill.

Library of Congress Cataloging-in-Publication Data
Arneson, Steve.
   Bootstrap leadership : 50 ways to break out, take charge, and move up / Steve Arneson ; foreword by Dave Ulrich.
      p. cm.
   Includes bibliographical references and index.
   ISBN 978-1-60509-345-1 (pbk. : alk. paper) 1. Leadership. 2. Executive ability. 3. Success in business. I. Title.
   HD57.7.A76 2010
   158'.4—dc22   2009047634

First Edition
15 14 13 12 11 10   10 9 8 7 6 5 4 3 2

Cover design: MVB Design
Cover photo: © Oytun Karadayi/iStockphoto

For my Dad,
who taught me a thing or two about leadership.

Contents

Part Two:
Add Something New to Your Game

Contents

Part Five:
It's Not about You

Contents

Foreword

WE'LL KNOW IT when we see it. This line has been used by teachers on the lookout for a good paper, by friends trying to find the right gift, and by followers in search of good leaders. Most of us know intuitively what good leaders look, talk, and feel like. They inspire us with their vision. They motivate us with their call to action. They care for us by their words and deeds. They develop us by their confidence. They relate to us through their values.

Yet leaders don't just magically succeed. They need to combine certain foundational elements with the passion and discipline of continuous improvement. Yes, they need the building block skills, but they also need to keep learning, growing, and developing. That's the formula for success, and in this book, Steve Arneson provides a fascinating roadmap for leadership self-development, one that leaders at all levels can follow to improve their performance.

But what is it that leaders need to develop? In our work, we have synthesized and integrated the *content* of what effective leaders must know and do. We have identified five basic rules leaders must follow:

Rule 1: Shape the Future. Leaders who shape the future answer the question, "Where are we going?" And they make sure that those around them understand the direction as well. Strategists figure out where the organization needs to go to succeed, test their ideas pragmatically against current resources (money, people, organizational capabilities), and work with others to figure out how to get to the desired future. The rules for Strategists are about creating, defining, and delivering principles of what is possible.

Rule 2: Make Things Happen. Leaders who make things happen focus on the question, "How will we make sure we get there?" Executors translate strategy into action and put the systems in place for others to do the same. They understand how to make change happen, assign accountability, make key decisions, and delegate responsibility to others, all while ensuring teams work well together and keeping promises to multiple stakeholders. The rules for Executors revolve around the discipline for getting things done and the technical expertise for getting them done right.

Rule 3: Engage Today's Talent. Leaders who optimize talent answer the question, "Who goes with us on our business journey?" Talent Managers know how to identify, build, and engage talent to get results. They identify the skills required, recruit and engage talent, communicate extensively, and ensure that employees give their best effort. Talent Managers generate intense personal, professional, and organizational loyalty. The rules for Talent Managers center on resolutions to help people develop professionally for the good of the organization.

Rule 4: Build the Next Generation. Leaders who mold the future talent pool answer the question, "Who stays and sustains the organization for the next generation?" Talent Managers ensure short-term results through people, whereas Human Capital Developers ensure the organization has the long-term competencies required for future strategic success, thus ensuring the organization outlives any single individual. Just as good parents invest in helping their children succeed, Human Capital Developers help future leaders to be successful. Throughout the organization, they build a workforce plan focused on future talent, understand how to develop that talent, and help employees envision their future careers within the company. Human Capital Developers install rules that demonstrate a pledge to building the next generation of talent.

Rule 5: Invest in Yourself. At the heart of the Leadership Code[1]— literally and figuratively—is Personal Proficiency. Effective leaders cannot be reduced to what they know or what they do. Leaders are learners, drawing on lessons from successes, failures, assignments, books, classes, people, and life experiences. Passionate about their beliefs and interests, good leaders spend enormous personal energy and attention on what matters to them. Effective leaders inspire loyalty and goodwill in others because they act with integrity and trust. Decisive and impassioned, they are capable of bold and courageous moves. Confident in their ability to deal with situations, they can tolerate ambiguity. Through our work, we have determined that all leaders must excel in Personal Proficiency. Without the foundation of trust and credibility, leaders cannot ask others to follow them.

The Process of Becoming an Effective Leader

If these five rules are the content of what leaders must know and do, what Steve Arneson does in this outstanding book is to lay out the *process* of becoming an effective leader. There is a knowing-doing gap that sometimes keeps leaders from fulfilling their aspirations. Turning what we know about effective leadership into what leaders really *do* requires insight into how to make things happen and the discipline to actually do it. That's the wonderful thing about this book; it shows you how to make positive changes in your leadership style and behaviors.

This book offers fifty practical and realistic insights into the process of becoming a more effective leader. The insights are byte-size, digestible, and doable. They give any leader who aspires to be better a concrete place to start in making personal improvements. Let me offer some tips for using the insights in this book to help you become a better leader.

1. Have a mindset and commitment to learning. Leaders at all levels need to improve. One of the key predictors of any leader is the ability to learn. Learning means that the past informs the present, that the present is not constrained by the past, and that the future may differ from the present. Leaders as learners reflect, ask questions, experiment, and improve. They constantly ask questions such as:
   a. What worked and what did not work in the recent leadership episode?
   b. What did I do and how was it received by those I was leading?
   c. How can I be better?
   Read this book with a mindset and commitment to learn. Each chapter is an action item you might use to enhance your leadership capability.
2. Do an honest assessment of strengths and weaknesses. The assessment in the beginning of the book provides a lens to determine where you are strong and weak as a leader. We build on our strengths, but we have to neutralize our weaknesses. And, we have to build on our strengths that strengthen others. This book does not need to be read in a linear way. After taking the test, jump to a chapter that focuses on your strength. Ask yourself, "How can I use this strength to strengthen someone else?" Or, jump to a chapter that addresses a weakness and ask, "How can I improve on this weakness?"
3. Start with small successes. Someone made the statement, "By the inch it's a cinch, by the yard it's hard." Trite, but true. Improving leadership does not come by leaps and bounds, grand epiphanies that transform the world, but by small and cumulative

actions that build leadership a brick at a time. This book is probably best used (not just read) by reading a chapter and implementing its techniques. See how the ideas work in your daily routine. See how others respond to you when you do the things Steve suggests. Then, repeat the procedure for the next chapter.

4. See yourself through the eyes of others. Leaders matter, but leadership matters more. Leaders are individuals who set visions, execute for results, and organize resources. Leadership exists when leaders develop the next generation. Like good parenting, leaders have to nurture and invest in others. As a leader, help those you are working with so that they can someday replace and surpass you. Use this book to identify some of the areas where they can improve so that they have opportunities and successes beyond even yours.

Steve is a leadership coach. By using this book, you can feel that he's beside you or inside your head offering you wise and timely counsel on how you can improve yourself. Being an effective leader sometimes requires third-party coaching where your coach observes and encourages you. But sometimes you are your own best coach. When you self-coach you become aware of what you can and should do to help your organization reach its goals through people and processes. This book offers a marvelous blueprint for self-coaching. The specific tools and tips can be quickly assimilated and eventually acted on so that you can become a better leader. These rules of leadership coupled with the process for learning and mastering the rules will help you move forward with more insight and confidence.

Dave Ulrich
Alpine, Utah
November 2009

Preface

THROUGHOUT MY CAREER, I've been fortunate to work for some great leaders. Although each had a different style, they had one particular quality in common—they were all relentlessly focused on continuous learning. These leaders challenged me, gave me opportunities to grow, and provided the feedback I needed to keep improving. They were actively engaged in my development, taught me the business, mentored me, and pushed me to mature as a leader. Even more impressive was their commitment to their own development. These leaders were constantly working on their leadership; they were willing to admit that they didn't know everything and cared about how they were showing up as a leader. I loved working for these people.

I've also worked for my share of bad leaders. These leaders shared some common traits as well, although the list isn't very pretty. These leaders were interested in their own agenda or reputation rather than the development of their people. They cared exclusively about the work rather than the individuals doing it. They didn't add positive energy to the group; they drained it. These leaders tended to be closed off to feedback, clueless about how their style impacted others, and totally uninterested in reflecting on their own leadership. Needless to say, I didn't enjoy working for these leaders.

I wrote this book because I have a passion for helping leaders reach their full potential and get to the "great" side of the leadership continuum. I spent many years as the head of leadership development at some terrific companies, and I have seen hundreds of leaders achieve better results because they worked to improve aspects of their leadership. They cared about getting better and did something about it. Today, in my executive coaching practice, I continue to work with leaders who seek feedback, use that input to build focused development plans, and make a concerted effort to become more effective. I think you can do it too.

This book is about you and the choices you make to become a better leader. It's about you having the dedication and perseverance to pull yourself up by your own bootstraps and develop your leadership skills. It's about gathering and listening to feedback about where you can improve and then acting on it. There is something about being open to feedback and wanting to have an even greater impact that fuels the best leaders; they thrive on continuous improvement. In effect, the central question of this book is, "How can I become a better leader?" Every leader has the potential to improve—but you have to work at it. You have to want to get better if you're going to become a more effective leader. No one can do this for you—this is *your* responsibility. This is *your* journey of self-improvement.

Working to improve your leadership isn't just smart; it's also the right thing to do. You see, I believe that leadership is a privilege, but what you do with that obligation is up to you. Whether you work in a large company or a small organization, when you manage other people, you have an opportunity to change lives. I firmly believe that. But you can't positively impact others if you're not personally willing to keep learning and growing. Your obligation as a leader extends to how you're modeling your own development.

Preface

In my professional career, I've had many opportunities to lead teams of people, so I've been in the same position you're in today. And what a great place to be—leading people is one of the most rewarding and fun roles you can have in business. Leading a team of dedicated professionals can be an amazing experience, and I was lucky enough to have several high-performing teams. What we accomplished together was incredible, and I owe all of my success to the people who worked with me—they made me look good as a leader. Along the way, we taught each other, gave each other feedback, and took an interest in each other's development. I wasn't always the perfect boss; I know that. But I tried to never lose sight of the responsibility I had to be a role model for continuous learning, and many of the ideas in this book come from those experiences. I hope you'll find them useful as you plan your own leadership development.

How to Use This Book

Bootstrap Leadership is a how-to book of leadership self-development. Every idea, tool, and exercise in the book is designed to help you improve current skills or develop new ones. Most of the ideas and techniques don't require a budget, and all are things you can apply every day on the job. No matter your level of leadership, from entry-level supervisor to senior executive, there are ideas in this book that can help you become a better leader.

The book begins with an introduction that explains the importance of self-development and a leadership self-assessment that establishes a baseline for your leadership. The self-assessment is designed to help you focus on the specific chapters that might have the biggest impact for you. The rest of the book is divided into five major sections, each with a particular development focus.

Chapters 1–10 are a great place to start; these chapters help answer the question, "How are you showing up as a leader?" and help you discover specific development opportunities. After all, if you're going to improve your leadership, it helps to know what others think of your skills and behaviors. These chapters also give you ideas on how to think about your leadership journey and how to solicit (and apply) feedback from others about your leadership style.

Chapters 11–20 are all about adding something new to your game. This section offers advice and techniques for adding new skills to your leadership toolkit. All leaders need to be open to developing new aspects of their leadership style. The ideas in these chapters help you to stretch your skill set, making you a more reflective, well-rounded leader.

Chapters 21–30 encourage you to get curious about the world around you. This section explores diversity, innovation, and best practices for inspiration and new ideas. Leaders today need to be globally aware; they can't afford to focus just on their own company or industry. The ideas in these chapters aim to expand your horizons and are intended to spark additional questions that you can pursue with your own teams.

Chapters 31–40 ask you to push the envelope and step out of your Comfort Zone. This section challenges you to try new things as you expand your leadership presence in the organization. The best learning experiences are those that lie outside of your Comfort Zone, and the techniques in these chapters will push you to move beyond your normal routines and practices.

Chapters 41–50 remind you that, in the end, it's not about you—it's about your team. It's not the leader's job to create a long line of followers; rather, the leader should identify and build leaders for the next generation. These chapters help you identify opportunities to drive your team's learning and development to new heights.

The idea to include fifty different ideas in the book came from the desire to give you something new to experiment with every week of the year (allowing for a couple of weeks of vacation, of course—you need time to rest and reflect, too!). If you read the book from beginning to end, you might want to bookmark certain chapters and return to the ideas as you try out new techniques. If you want to skip around and try different ideas, take the self-assessment and read those chapters that correspond to your most critical development needs. Throughout the book, I've indicated where certain chapters refer to other chapters to help you link the various ideas. Regardless of how you use the book, you're sure to find tools and techniques that you can apply immediately. Ideally, you'll share some of the ideas with your direct reports to help them become more effective leaders, too.

If you are responsible for other people—at any level—then you are a leader. You owe it to them (and yourself) to be continuously improving your skills. You've already done the easy part; you picked up this book. Now, roll up your sleeves and get to work—take charge of your own leadership development, and start pulling yourself up by your own bootstraps!

Steve Arneson
Leesburg, Virginia
November 2009

Introduction

CONGRATULATIONS ON THE DECISION to develop yourself into a more effective leader! You are about to embark on an exciting journey, one that will reward you with more knowledge, improved skills, and enhanced maturity as a leader. By picking up this book, you've decided to take charge of your own leadership development and, in the process, create your own personalized learning agenda. Given today's economic climate and pace of change, you can't wait for the organization to bring leadership training to you; you have to be willing to work on your own game. You can't rely solely on your boss for coaching and mentoring; you need to take charge of your own growth as a leader. And you certainly can't take just one class a year and consider that your development plan. No, you need a broader, deeper learning strategy and a customized plan of action. In short, you need to pull yourself up by your own bootstraps. And you need to do it now.

If You're Not Moving Forward, You're Moving Backward

We are living in extraordinary times. The world is becoming more complicated every day, and we are becoming increasingly reliant on one key ingredient, at all levels of business and society, to help us make sense of the complexities. That critical factor is leadership. Whether it's the relentless march of technology, global competitiveness, sustainability, or innovation, strong leadership has never been in greater demand. But you know this, because you're living it. You're on the front lines—connecting with customers, reducing costs, creating green strategies, and motivating and inspiring your employees. If you're a leader (at any level) in an organization today—whether a large or small company, a professional services firm, a school, or a nonprofit or government agency—you must continue to learn and grow or you won't keep up. No matter where you are, if you don't take charge of your development, who will?

Make no mistake: It's competitive out there, and one of the ways to stay ahead of the competition is to constantly develop your skills. Think of it this way: How would you like to come to work tomorrow with the same skills you had ten years ago? Most of us wouldn't last a day! As you're well aware, right behind you are plenty of bright, aggressive managers who would love to move up and take your place. If you're not willing to evolve as a leader, they certainly are. So what's it going to be?

The fact is, if you manage people or have a leadership role in your organization, you have to constantly add new capabilities to your toolkit. This isn't about maintaining the status quo anymore—things have changed. This is about you staying ahead of the curve and developing your leadership skills so you'll be ready for challenges that you haven't even dreamed of yet. This is about taking control of your own development and establishing your own leadership brand—one that says: "I care about becoming a better leader."

What's Your Legacy?

Why lead at all? What's so remarkable about being a leader? There are many ways to contribute in this world that have nothing to do with leading people. While that's true, there's something magical about being the driving force that helps a group of people accomplish something extraordinary. My philosophy on leadership is that it's all about the people, not the task. Yes, you're trying to get stuff done; that's why the team or organization exists. But leaders don't lead buildings or computer systems or budgets; they lead people. For me, leadership is about helping others to be the best they can be.

In my coaching practice, I often pose this question to senior executives: "What do you want your legacy to be?" It's a popular question, yet many leaders struggle to answer it. Generally, if they have a response, it's something along the lines of, "Someone who got things done and took care of his people along the way." OK, that's a pretty good answer. But unless you've invented something pretty amazing or orchestrated a big merger, no one's going to remember your specific results; what they will remember is what it felt like to work with you. Don't believe me? What were you working on five years ago this month? How about two years ago? Does that brilliant spreadsheet or PowerPoint presentation jump right to mind? How about this one: Who was your boss two years ago? Who was on your team two years ago? Easier to remember, yes? The fact is, most people will remember your leadership in visceral terms (what it felt like to work for you) rather than a list of your specific accomplishments.

Here's an illustration of what I mean. When I facilitate leadership development programs, I ask the participants to go through a "best boss/worst boss" exercise. I put the participants in small groups and ask them to share stories about the best boss they have ever had and how these leaders made them feel. Their answers are almost all about personal connections; how the boss challenged, coached, empowered, and enabled them to succeed. You can feel the positive energy in the room as people share stories of bosses who helped them grow and develop. The mood shifts, though, when they share stories of the worst boss they ever had; metaphorically, it's like a shadow has been cast over the room. I've heard some really depressing bad boss stories, and they mainly have to do with people being ignored, humiliated, or mistreated by their boss. The common denominator is clear: "They didn't care about me as a person."

How do you want to be remembered by your direct reports? As one of their best bosses ever, or as the bad punch line in a "worst boss I ever had" story? It's up to you. Are you establishing a compelling vision and creating a winning strategy? Are you setting a high bar for excellence? Are you challenging your people to grow and develop? Are you delegating effectively, so you can spend your time leading as opposed to doing? Are you stretching your leadership across the organization? If the answer is "not as well as I could be," then read this book. It will help point you in the right direction.

Improve Something Every Day

It is possible to get a little better each day as a leader. If you're willing to put in the time, you really can learn, practice, and apply new skills (or polish established ones) on a consistent basis. Your evolution as a leader never ends; you can always gain more wisdom, patience and maturity. You can always become a better listener or a more effective coach. And the more you grow, the more confidence you'll gain as a leader. As you gain confidence, you'll be willing to keep improving, and that will make you a more effective leader. Growth, confidence, effectiveness—now that's a winning formula that you can get excited about! You can do this; you can take your leadership to a higher level and, in the process, grow and develop your team, too. Start by taking the following self-assessment, and start putting together your own customized leadership development plan!

Bootstrap Leadership:
Self-Assessment

Bootstrap Leadership includes fifty ideas, tools, and techniques for developing your leadership skills. Because every leader has different strengths and opportunities, this self-assessment is designed to help you identify which chapters of the book target your particular development needs.

Circle the rating that best describes your response to each item, and consult the scoring guide for recommended sections and chapters that can help you break out, take charge, and move up.

	Not At All	Somewhat			Definitely
1. I remember where, when, and how I learned my leadership lessons.	1	2	3	4	5
2. I have a clear sense of my professional network (work relationships).	1	2	3	4	5
3. I know how my peers and direct reports would rate me as a leader.	1	2	3	4	5
4. I have no trouble staying disciplined when it comes to personal development.	1	2	3	4	5
5. Mentors have played a big role in my development as a leader.	1	2	3	4	5
6. I regularly consult with a group of peers about my development.	1	2	3	4	5
7. I pay attention to and leverage my strengths.	1	2	3	4	5
8. My colleagues from past organizations keep me motivated to learn and grow.	1	2	3	4	5

	Not At All		Somewhat		Definitely
9. I'm open-minded and willing to see all sides of an issue.	1	2	3	4	5
10. My team has a clear sense of why we exist and what we're trying to do.	1	2	3	4	5
11. I believe it's important to have a personal definition of leadership.	1	2	3	4	5
12. I keep a detailed leadership development plan.	1	2	3	4	5
13. My approach to learning new skills involves deep immersion into the subject.	1	2	3	4	5
14. I do a good job of delegating tasks to my team.	1	2	3	4	5
15. My peers and direct reports would say I'm a good coach.	1	2	3	4	5
16. I find value in reading the latest business books.	1	2	3	4	5
17. I record my leadership reflections in a journal.	1	2	3	4	5
18. I do my homework to understand some of the underlying theories of leadership.	1	2	3	4	5
19. I tell a lot of stories when communicating with my team or others.	1	2	3	4	5
20. My personal values are clear to everyone who works with me.	1	2	3	4	5
21. I am familiar with my employees' cultural backgrounds.	1	2	3	4	5

	Not At All	Somewhat		Definitely	

22. I have a good working knowledge of the different parts of my organization.   1   2   3   4   5

23. I keep close tabs on my professional network.   1   2   3   4   5

24. I do my own research to stay up to date on the latest leadership trends.   1   2   3   4   5

25. I take a keen interest in my people's personal lives.   1   2   3   4   5

26. I believe there is value in regularly meeting with vendors and consultants.   1   2   3   4   5

27. I know the impact our major competitors have on our company.   1   2   3   4   5

28. I stay up to date on other organizations' best practices.   1   2   3   4   5

29. One of my leadership passions is innovation.   1   2   3   4   5

30. I find ways to relate lessons outside of work to my leadership development.   1   2   3   4   5

---

31. I am willing to try new behaviors and other ways of doing things.   1   2   3   4   5

32. I regularly admit my shortcomings and limitations.   1   2   3   4   5

33. I'm open to attending local networking events.   1   2   3   4   5

34. I'm comfortable speaking to other groups in the organization about my team.   1   2   3   4   5

35. I'm comfortable asking my boss for new and different assignments.   1   2   3   4   5

	Not At All	Somewhat	Definitely

36. I am comfortable reading my organization's financial statements.   1 2 3 4 5

37. I'm confident in my ability to build a compelling business case.   1 2 3 4 5

38. I know how my health affects my performance and productivity.   1 2 3 4 5

39. I can imagine myself in a different leadership role.   1 2 3 4 5

40. I'm open to having my team critique our products and services.   1 2 3 4 5

41. I am satisfied with how I showcase my team to senior management.   1 2 3 4 5

42. I enjoy volunteering my time and expertise to groups outside of work.   1 2 3 4 5

43. I'm comfortable giving feedback to my boss and peers.   1 2 3 4 5

44. I spend quality time with my direct reports' teams.   1 2 3 4 5

45. I spend my leadership time efficiently, focused on the right big things.   1 2 3 4 5

46. I am open to teaching a formal training course inside the organization.   1 2 3 4 5

47. I spend time reflecting on my leadership impact.   1 2 3 4 5

48. I pitch in on leadership tasks outside of my regular duties.   1 2 3 4 5

49. I pay attention and listen carefully when having conversations with others.   1 2 3 4 5

50. I'm preparing for the day when I move on to a new leadership position.   1 2 3 4 5

Bootstrap Leadership:
Self-Assessment Scoring Guide

Items in the self-assessment correspond directly to the fifty *Bootstrap Leadership* chapters. For example, item 35 represents the content found in Chapter 35, and so on. For items you rated a 1, 2, or 3, focus on the corresponding chapters to find tips, ideas, and recommendations for improving your leadership skills.

You can also target your development needs on a broader level by looking at how you rated yourself across the ten items that make up one of the following categories:

Items 1–10: *How Are You Showing Up as a Leader?*
- This section includes ideas for gathering input and feedback about your leadership style.

Items 11–20: *Add Something New to Your Game*
- This section includes recommendations for adding new skills to your leadership toolkit.

Items 21–30: *Get Curious about the World Around You*
- This section is about adding a new perspective and looking past the four walls of your office.

Items 31–40: *Step Out of Your Comfort Zone*
- This section challenges you to take a risk and break out of your normal routine.

Items 41–50: *It's Not about You*
- This section offers you ideas for making your leadership all about others.

Part One

How Are You
Showing Up as a Leader?

SO YOU'VE DECIDED to get serious about working on your leadership game. That's great— given everything that's going on in the world today, you've made a wise choice to continue developing your skills. But how should you begin this journey? Here's a hint: How about finding out what others think of you as a leader? While you're excited about your own development, the fact is there are lots of other people who have something to gain if you improve your leadership skills—people such as your peers, your boss, and most important, your team members. How about checking in with them to see how you're showing up as a leader? Seems like a logical place to start, right? In fact, asking others for feedback is the "start" square on the game board of leadership development.

As you consider which areas to work on, ask the people around you for input. How are they experiencing your leadership? What's working for them? What's not working? How do they feel about your ability to guide the team in the right direction? What suggestions do they have for taking your skills to the next level? If you're sincere about soliciting and listening to their feedback, they'll tell you what you need to work on.

But it's not just others that you need to consult—you need to have a few honest conversations with yourself, too. Where has your career taken you? What have you learned along the way? What opinions have you formed that are helping you to succeed or, maybe, setting you up for a fall? What do you do really well, and what do you know you still need to develop? Can you trust yourself to diligently work on new behaviors, or are you going to need some assistance? What about the quality of your relationships? Where do you have opportunities to leverage the people around you for support on this journey?

This section of the book helps you find the answers to these questions. Start by inviting others to give you feedback and by reflecting on your own leadership brand (i.e., how others perceive you as a leader). If you want to break out and take charge of your own leadership development, this is the place to start. Take a deep breath, keep an open mind, and start pulling yourself up by your own bootstraps!

1

Where Have You Been?

Document Your Leadership Journey

"IF YOU DON'T KNOW where you're going, any road will take you there." I love this quote, not only because it's supposed to get you moving if you're stuck, but also because it screams, "Get organized, and have a plan!" This is great advice whether you're planning a trip or your own leadership development. Any significant journey worth taking is worth planning. Let's pretend you're taking a six-month sabbatical to climb Mount Everest. You wouldn't dream of tackling this adventure without a lot of planning, right? You also wouldn't plan this trip without looking back at what you've learned from other high-peak ascents, both successful and unsuccessful. You're going to need every bit of that experience to make this climb, so you better take stock of your lessons learned. The fact is that looking back can help you see the next adventure more clearly.

The same is true when it comes to planning the next step in your journey of leadership self-discovery. One of the first things you should do is reflect on where you've been as a leader. Are you doing this on a regular basis? Are you reflecting on your lessons learned? You should be; the leader who doesn't learn from his or her mistakes is doomed to repeat them. What were the critical moments that shaped you as a manager? How did you react? What did you do well, and what could you have done better? How did others respond to you? When did you start to feel like a true leader? Most important, what did you learn from these moments?

Leadership is definitely a personal experience; the lessons you learn may be common ones, but the specifics of each situation make your leadership story unique. All of us can remember critical incidents that shaped us as leaders—times when we learned from a mistake or stepped up in a big way. Maybe it was standing up to a boss when you knew you were right. Maybe it was failing to pull the trigger on a bad hire or supporting an employee who turned out to be a star. Or maybe it was really listening to feedback and recognizing that you needed to change your leadership style.

Some lessons involve other people and can reveal patterns, such as failing to leverage peers or build relationships. Other lessons involve your own judgment—a fateful read of the strategy that leads to poor decisions or opportunities seized because you were willing to take a calculated risk. Your career is filled with times when you made the right call, did the right thing, or learned a difficult lesson. These are the touchstones of your life as a leader, the milestones along your leadership path. Your own leadership journey provides tremendous insight into how you should continue developing as a leader. In other words, where you've been can help clarify where you need to go. By reflecting on your lessons learned, you can build a development plan that optimizes your remaining growth areas.

Write Your Own Leadership Journey

There is an easy way to document your lessons and build your leadership story. Start with your first leadership role, when you first began to manage people. Write down the company, your job title, and the time frame you were in the role. Remember when you got your first direct report to manage? Were you excited about the opportunity? Maybe a little intimidated by the responsibility? You probably did several things right; but you might have made a few mistakes, too—first-time supervisors usually do. Think back to that job. What were the two or three most critical incidents that happened in that role, and what were the most profound learnings from those experiences? Write them down. Take the time to really think about the experience, but capture the essence of the lesson in a few simple words. Now, go on to your next role and repeat the process. At the end of this exercise, you should have traced your entire career as a leader and recorded your critical incidents and lessons learned along the way (see Figure 1).

Put your leadership story on a PowerPoint slide or practice telling it from memory. Share it with your boss, your peers, and your team. If you have a large organization, share it with your entire department in an all-hands meeting. Sharing your leadership journey allows you to model three powerful leadership tools at once: reflection, storytelling, and lifelong learning. Take your audience through your career, and tell the stories that have molded your leadership philosophy. Stories make your lessons come alive and cast you in a favorable light, as they generally involve you having learned from mistakes. Share your journey with pride—these are lessons that have had a profound impact on you, and sharing them candidly demonstrates that you're open to learning from the lessons that lie ahead.

In my career, I've helped dozens of leaders create and present their leadership journeys, and the process has been beneficial every time. People love the framework because it helps them establish authenticity, which is critical for leaders. The process is particularly effective with leaders who have a reputation for being "hard to read" because the personal journey tends to showcase them as regular people. Sometimes, the leaders I work with are reluctant to build a robust story; they think they're bragging about their background or, worse yet, aren't proud of some of their career choices. The fact is, your journey is your journey—those are the stops you made along the way. Don't apologize for them. Every experience helped shape who you are today. Besides, the more important stories involve critical incidents and lessons learned—the very instances you should emphasize and use to grab the audience's attention.

By studying where you've been, and what you've learned, you can better chart the course of your future development. What leadership lessons do you still need to learn? What traps do you want to avoid? What experiences do you need to add to your story? Reflect on your own journey by writing and telling your leadership story, and you'll create a more vivid roadmap for self-development going forward.

Bootstrap
Takeaways

Document Your Leadership Journey

1. Create your own leadership story by mapping your critical experiences and lessons learned. Pick out the memorable moments and be specific.

2. Share your leadership journey with others—practice telling your story.

3. Use the past to plan the future—what do you still need (and want) to learn?

2

Build a Spider Web

Evaluate Your Working Relationships

WORK IS BASICALLY A SERIES of relationships. Everyone you work with represents a distinct connection, and collectively your connections represent your working network. Because networks are fluid, every time you interact with someone you have a chance to build a stronger relationship, and when you meet someone new, you have the opportunity to add to your network. A strong network can help advance your career. So are you doing everything you can to build your network? What's that? You're too busy to work on your professional network? I used to say that too. I was focused on getting work done, not meeting or reconnecting with colleagues and peers. I didn't have time for people that weren't in my immediate line of sight. But that's a mistake that can have major consequences. We all need to pay attention to our networks, because we never know when we're going to need them.

Every day you have dozens of chances to turn acquaintances into colleagues, colleagues into friends, and friends into true business partners that will help you succeed. There's no question about it—relationships matter, especially for leaders who have to get things done. The more high-quality relationships you have, the more effective you'll be as a leader. You need these people to be successful, because you can't wave a magic wand and invent an entirely new network (unless of course you leave your job and start fresh elsewhere—but that's a subject for a future chapter).

Assess the Quality of Your Relationships

Here's a simple exercise to assess the quality of your relationships, and in turn, determine where you have work to do to further your development as a leader. Draw the following web diagram on a large sheet of paper: Write your name in the middle of a rectangle and draw five increasingly larger rings around it on the page. Label the outermost ring "Excellent" and the corresponding rings (moving toward the center of the page) as follows: "Very Good," "Good," "OK," and "Poor." Now, consider the people you know and place them somewhere on the diagram. Go deep into your network when doing this exercise; list everyone you can think of. The typical leader might have up to forty or fifty names on the diagram. Your best friend with whom you eat lunch every day goes on the "Excellent" ring. You seem to have clicked with that new colleague—put her on the "Good" ring for now. The manager in your department that you always seem to be competing with—be honest, you probably could improve that relationship; better put him in the "Poor" category. That vendor that has helped build your internal reputation goes in the "Very Good" ring. The key to this exercise is to be brutally honest with yourself; don't overinflate your ratings.

As you add names to the web, do so in three different colors. Use one color for operational relationships, to indicate those colleagues you work with on a regular basis. These would include people on your own teams, within your department, and so on. Use another color to indicate strategic relationships—people within the organization that you interact with to get things done (those in Purchasing, Finance, HR, Business Development, etc.). Finally, use a third color for external business relationships (partners, vendors, customers, clients, etc.). After you've added all of your existing relationships, list the people in the company that you should know but don't. Maybe you have a casual "hi in the hallways" relationship or know who they are but just haven't met them yet. Write their names in the far corners of the page, without plotting them on the web (after all, you don't have a relationship with them yet).

What Is the Web Diagram Telling You?

Once finished, step back and analyze the diagram for trends and patterns. Where do you have the strongest relationships? If it's in the operational area, you may be overly comfortable within your own functional area and may not be stretching your network across the organization. If it's in the strategic area, you're influencing well throughout the company, but you may struggle a bit over direction, philosophy, and so forth within your own group. If it's in the external business area, then you're clearly focused outside the enterprise, which may mean you're more comfortable establishing relationships at a distance or have strong relationships from previous roles. Note the number of relationships that are just "OK" or "Poor." What can you do to improve these relationships? Make a specific action plan for each relationship, with a goal of moving each one at least one ring farther out in the next thirty days. Where do you want to establish relationships that don't exist today? Make a specific plan to meet those people or work with them on a project, for example. For both action plans, indicate how adding or improving these relationships will make you a better leader.

If you're not looking at your work relationships as a resource, you should be. Relationships need to be nurtured and developed, like any other skill or asset. This is not something you're going to learn in a class or read in a book, and the organization isn't going to do it for you. Establishing and nurturing relationships is something you have to do. As you think about developing yourself as a leader, you're going to lean on these people for help and feedback. Look at the web as a metaphor for the strength of your leadership brand—the stronger your relationships, the stronger your reputation as a leader is likely to be across the organization.

Assess the quality of your relationships and make a concerted effort to improve the most critical ones lower on the scale. This simple process might be the most important self-evaluation exercise you do all year. Because while you're busy pulling yourself up by your own bootstraps, it doesn't hurt to have a strong network of colleagues pulling with you!

Bootstrap
Takeaways

Evaluate Your Working Relationships

1. Plot the quality of your relationships. Be honest—place people where they really belong on the diagram.
2. YOU are responsible for investing in and managing your relationships. Strive to move the lowest rated relationships out one ring in the next thirty days.
3. Do this exercise once a year, and set goals for adding new names to the diagram.

3

Spin Around in a Circle

Make 360° Feedback Work for You

HAVING CAPTURED YOUR LEADERSHIP lessons and analyzed your working relationships, you're ready to take the next step: gathering feedback from others on how they're experiencing your leadership. Do you know what others think of your leadership style? What are your strengths and opportunities as a leader? How do others really feel about working for you? Do you know the answers to these questions? You may think you do. But there's only one way to find out for sure. There's an old leadership adage that says "If you want to know how well you're leading, turn around and see if anyone's following you." You'll never get the full picture of your leadership if you're always looking forward. From time to time, you need to turn around and make sure your people are still behind you. And while you're at it, try to get a sense of their feelings about your leadership.

This is the idea behind the greatest leadership assessment tool ever invented: 360° feedback. The 360° process involves a formal collection of input from your direct reports, peers, and managers on your leadership style and behaviors. The feedback is generally gathered using a quantitative survey, and most 360° tools involve the solicitation of written comments, which are usually presented anonymously. The data and the written comments are compiled into a comprehensive, personalized report (generally by a professional consulting firm), which is then given to you and debriefed, typically by a human resources or leadership development professional. Whether it's conducted formally or informally, the 360° process is a great way to confirm what you're doing right, discover possible blind spots, and get suggestions for improving your leadership skills. It's hard to think of a more efficient and effective assessment process.

Getting the Most Out of Your 360° Feedback

Looking at your leadership through the eyes of others demands courage and a willingness to absorb some potentially negative feedback. The first time you get 360° feedback can be a little scary, frankly. It's natural to be somewhat defensive about the data, initially. I remember staring at the cover of my first 360° feedback report and feeling nervous about opening it. I was definitely worried about what others had to say about me. However, once I started to absorb the data and read the written comments, I relaxed and started to appreciate the feedback. Turns out I was doing many things right, but I also got a lot of useful, constructive feedback that helped me to improve. I've now completed the 360° process several times, and each time it has proven extremely helpful in directing my continued development. Whether you're in a large company or a small organization, you have to be willing to look in the mirror and find out how you're showing up as a leader. It can be frightening, no doubt—and you probably won't like everything people have to say about you. Recognize that this is normal; try to push through it and accept the feedback for what it is: the reality of how others experience your leadership.

The bottom line is that 360° feedback can be one of your best development experiences if you commit to four fundamental principles. First, you have to select people who will provide brutally honest feedback. Ask your manager to help you choose a variety of raters; the key is to go beyond selecting just those who will say great things about you. Be sure to include people you've had a few disagreements with in the past so that you get an accurate, well-rounded view of your leadership style. Yes, that means the person down the hall that you don't exactly get along with; if you're going to do this effectively, you need to go all in. When you request feedback, ask your respondents to be as honest as possible, and thank them afterward for their input.

Second, you need to keep an open mind and really listen to the feedback. Review the numerical charts, and look for patterns and nuances in the data. Strengths can be leveraged to develop weaknesses, so don't discount what respondents say you do well—learning what others think you're exceptional at is just as important as learning what they think you need to improve on. Look closely at how different rater groups respond; you may be showing up as a leader in one way to your peers and in a completely different way to your direct reports. Be aware of blind spots—areas where you feel you're effective, yet others disagree. Finally, read the written comments carefully. Typically, this is where the truth lies; the context and real-world examples make the feedback come alive, and you can learn a lot from the level of passion that goes into these comments. Be aware that your first reaction is likely to be defensive, which can easily close you off to some very important development suggestions. Remember that feedback is a gift; you need to see it as an opportunity to improve, not as something to be avoided or discounted.

Third, be sure to turn the feedback into an actionable development plan. Pinpoint the two or three highest priority development areas that you want to improve, and identify specific behaviors that others rated either the same or differently than you did (see Figure 2). Type up your development plan, share it with your boss, and ask for coaching as you work toward your improvement goals. It's difficult for others to notice improvement if you haven't told them what you're going to be working on, so share the plan with your direct reports and peers, too. The best way to make significant improvement is to communicate your stated goals (for more on development plans, see Chapter 12).

Finally, ask for support and continued feedback from your immediate network. Thank your raters and request ongoing input as you work on your new leadership behaviors. Give them permission to call you on a lack of effort or a regression from your desired development path. Ask your boss about the 360° feedback process in your organization. If the tool is available, volunteer to go through the process. If your organization doesn't currently utilize this tool, ask HR or your manager to help you access one of the many excellent 360° instruments available online. If that's not possible, ask a few of your close colleagues for direct feedback— simply ask: "How can I be a better leader?"

If you've done a 360°, you know how valuable the process can be. If you haven't, give it a try—you won't regret it. After all, you can't develop yourself in a vacuum; you need other people to give you feedback and support your plans for improvement. Besides, it's one of the best ways of finding out if anyone's truly following your leadership!

Bootstrap
Takeaways

Make 360° Feedback Work for You

1. Initiate a 360° process for yourself to establish a baseline of your leadership style and behaviors.
2. Pay close attention to what people say about you—manage your defensiveness and embrace the feedback!
3. Thank your feedback providers and enlist them in your development plan going forward. Give people a reason to root for you by being a gracious recipient of their input.

4

Your Own Private Detective

Ask a Peer to Track Your Development

LET'S SAY YOU'VE IDENTIFIED a particularly difficult development challenge for yourself. It might have surfaced from the 360° process, or maybe your boss has really started to insist that you shore up a particular weakness (those darn bosses—they do that sometimes, don't they?). OK, because you're incredibly perceptive, you've figured out that he's serious this time; you need to work on this behavior, or else. You're not sure what the "or else" is, but you're not willing to find out. You're ready to turn this around—right now. You're going to plot your own self-development and make this weakness disappear for good.

So, you're committed . . . but there's one little problem. You know this is going to be a tough assignment. Especially under stress, you are worried that you'll slip back into your old ways of doing things. Basically, you don't trust yourself; you know this skill is going to be hard to master. Sound familiar? Well, if this behavior change is that important, you need a safety net—a method for ensuring that you stay on track.

One way to create a fail-safe monitoring system is to ask a peer or a colleague to track your progress in a particular development area. Ask your colleague to give you regular feedback about what you're doing well and where you can still improve. Find someone you can trust to give you an honest assessment, who can track your progress in terms of driving positive behavior change. Think of this person as your own private detective, one you've hired to keep an eye on you while you build new skills.

Whomever you choose, he or she needs to be ready and willing to help and must be present when you demonstrate these new skills. The specific development challenge will dictate who you enlist for the watchdog role. For example, if your improvement opportunity involves changing your behavior in staff meetings, your detective needs to be a peer who's present in those meetings. If you need to show more leadership presence when presenting to your manager's peers or other senior leaders, then your manager is the right person to ask for feedback. If you are trying to talk less and listen more in your own staff meetings, then identify and "deputize" one of your direct reports to watch for the right behaviors. Regardless of who your detective is, you need to ask for feedback immediately after an event to determine whether or not you are demonstrating the desired behaviors.

An example from my own experience illustrates the value of this technique. A long time ago I had a boss that I really struggled to connect with, and because I was young and somewhat immature (I know, you can't possibly relate to this story), I did not always keep my composure when he said something outrageous in our staff meetings. My facial expressions (or maybe it was the long, deep sighs?) gave me away every time; it was clear by looking at me that I thought he was a complete idiot. Fortunately, one of my peers told me that I was over the line and offered to kick me under the table every time I outwardly displayed negativity. Over time, it worked. I shaped up, and with the help of my trusted colleague, I responded to my boss in a mature and appropriate manner. Looking back now, I realize I was lucky to have someone who was willing to point out my flaws and help me through the change process. Without that feedback and assistance, I might have continued down a very dangerous path. As it turns out, I'm living proof that this technique works.

Establish Three Key Agreements

When "hiring" your private eye, be specific about three elements of the assignment. First, be sure your detective understands exactly what it is you're trying to enhance or change. Explain the development challenge, and discuss any parameters associated with time, place, and frequency. In other words, make sure your detective knows what to look for and how to recognize the specific nuances of the behaviors, body language, speech, etc. Second, stress that you want your detective to be as specific as possible when documenting your behavior and recording feedback. For instance, if you're trying to reduce the number of times you say "umm" before speaking, agree that your detective will literally keep a running count that he or she will review with you later. If you want help to correct inappropriate body language or facial expressions, ask your detective to keep a count and a description. Finally, make it clear that you want constructive feedback, unfiltered and unvarnished. Ask your detective to "give it to you straight" and agree not to take the feedback personally. You've asked your detective to watch your every move in this specific area, and you need to let him or her play that role. If you are caught doing a poor job, you need to hear the negative feedback and make adjustments. If your detective notices that you are meeting most of your objectives, that's great; accept the positive feedback graciously and ask for suggestions on how you can be even *more* effective. Your goal isn't always to turn an area of concern into a strength, but you need to at least move it to the neutral zone so it's not impeding your progress as a leader. You do want to avoid the dreaded "or else," right?

Working together with your detective, you should make significant progress toward achieving your development goals. If you're trying to modify an everyday behavior, ask your detective to monitor you closely for a full month. When it seems you have turned the corner on this specific behavior, relieve your partner of his or her feedback role. Give your detective a small gift of appreciation, and thank him or her for helping keep you on track. Offer to reciprocate roles, and share this technique with others throughout the company.

The practice of asking a close friend, peer, or colleague to keep close tabs on your behavior is a wonderful technique for helping you cement your development efforts. If you're going to use this approach, though, do it with obvious behaviors that others can readily observe; it doesn't work as well for changes you're trying to make in your attitude or thinking skills. However, the next time you have a challenging, *visible* behavior change ahead of you, consider asking someone to help keep you on track; you'll find that constant and honest feedback from a trusted co-worker is just what you need to make the new behavior a permanent part of your leadership style.

Bootstrap
Takeaways

Ask a Peer to Track Your Development

1. Identify someone you can trust to monitor your progress on a specific developmental opportunity.
2. Ask for honest, constructive feedback, and accept it without debate. Then, use the input to improve.
3. Use this technique for visible behavior change where you know you need direct feedback and constant reinforcement.

5

When the Student Is Ready

Find a Mentor

THE GREAT THING ABOUT developing yourself as a leader is that you don't have to make the journey alone. There is an ancient Buddhist proverb that says: "When the student is ready, the teacher will appear." Loosely interpreted, this means that when you're open and willing to listen, you will find the answers from someone who has been down the road before you. In the modern business world, this proverb is best defined as mentoring.

It's easy to confuse mentoring with its popular first cousin, executive coaching. There are, however, some big differences between coaching and mentoring. Coaching facilitates the self-discovery process and involves working with someone who is skilled at asking questions to unlock your own insights. Mentors, however, provide more explicit advice and counsel and likely will be trusted members of your network, either inside or outside the organization. Essentially, a coach helps you find your own answers, whereas a mentor not only answers your questions but also offers specific recommendations. Both techniques are ideal for helping you develop as a leader (for a deeper dive into coaching, see Chapter 15). For now, let's take a closer look at mentoring, including how to use this development technique and how to get the most out of the relationship.

The Mentor Is a Teacher

Mentors are like teachers in that they give advice and help you learn new knowledge and skills. They counsel you on decisions and have a definite view of any situation or scenario you bring them. If you ask a coach, "What should I do here?" they're going to say: "What do *you* think you should do?" Ask a mentor that question, and you're going to get a specific answer, maybe more than one! The mentor sees it as his or her job to actively help you sort through options and alternative responses.

How do you pick a mentor? Well, sometimes a mentor picks you, of course. If you're lucky enough to have someone more experienced looking out for you and giving you advice, you're in great shape. If a senior leader in the organization (especially one who commands a lot of respect) wants to spend time with you, by all means, accept the offer. On three occasions in my career, I was fortunate to have senior executives (who were not my immediate bosses) take an interest in my development and invite me to tap into their knowledge and expertise. Although we didn't set up a formal schedule of meetings, I would call or visit them when crucial leadership decisions or career choices presented themselves. I just knew I'd be more confident about my plan of action if I was able to talk it over with my mentor ahead of time. I even spent a day shadowing one of my mentors to get a sense for his leadership presence and impact on others. I knew he spent a lot of time moving from meeting to meeting, and I wanted to see firsthand how he maintained his energy and enthusiasm. At the end of the day we debriefed and discussed his approach, and I learned some valuable lessons—not the least of which was his practice of quietly meditating for two to three minutes before walking into a meeting. In his office, he would close his eyes for a moment and clear his mind before moving to the next session; he told me it allowed him to let go of the previous meeting and focus on the next one.

I never forgot that lesson; and although it's something you can read about, it means more when you see a senior leader that you admire doing it!

So yes, it's great if a mentor finds you. But a lot of times you need to be the one asking for assistance. The key is to seek out someone who has knowledge or experience in the specific area where you most need help. Figure out where you're struggling or where you could use some guidance. Then ask someone who's been there or has a unique perspective to spend some time with you. The easiest way to do this is to approach them head on with the question. Simply say: "I have a lot of respect for what you've accomplished here and would love to tap into your knowledge and experience. Would you be willing to spend time with me to give me some advice and share your expertise?" Most senior leaders are more than happy to help and will readily say yes.

Mentors come in all varieties: Sometimes it's a former manager or colleague that you've stayed in touch with for years. Perhaps it's an executive in your organization. Often times, it's a peer—someone with whom you've always had a strong relationship. In most cases, you never formally enter into a "mentoring contract"; it's just understood that you respect this person and will continue to seek their counsel. Other times, the organization will literally match you with a mentor. In either case, your mentor is someone who has the experience and maturity to help you make important decisions.

Regardless of your connection, there are three elements that need to exist for mentoring to be productive for both parties. First, you need to trust your mentor's advice, otherwise, there's no point in listening to it. You have to find a mentor who will tell you the truth and has your best interests at heart; when seeking a mentor, make it clear that you want their honest assessment at all times. Second, although the mentoring relationship doesn't have to be formal, you should be clear about what you want when you ask for your mentor's input. Are you just looking to brainstorm with someone, or are you really interested in this person's suggestions? Don't make your mentor guess what you want; make your requests clear. Finally, you don't have to follow your mentor's advice, but you do need to be gracious and say thank you. The mentor is in this because he or she likes you or wants to see you succeed. Don't abuse the relationship; asking your mentor if there is anything you can do in return is a nice way to keep the mutual admiration society going.

Leverage Your Mentors

What's the best way to use a mentor? There are several ways, and all of them have to do with your continuous development as a leader. First, sometimes you just need to ask someone: *"How am I showing up as a leader?"* (the key question from Chapter 1). Asking your trusted mentor for the straight scoop can be a safe way to get feedback on your leadership style and behaviors. Second, your mentor can give you specific advice if you're struggling with a project or a relationship. They can help you prepare for difficult conversations, plan for a big presentation, or work through a complicated problem. If they work in your company, they can be particularly useful in helping you navigate the cultural and political landscape, especially higher up in the organization. Finally, mentors can be a great source of advice on career choices. If you're contemplating a move or a new assignment, don't make a final decision without checking in with your mentor.

Unlike a formal coach, whom you might use only once or twice in your entire career, a mentor is useful on an everyday basis. You should always have one or two mentors and should be tapping into them on a regular basis. If you find yourself asking: "I wonder what Bill or Mary would say about this" it's probably time to ask for a bit of advice. Even if you're pretty sure what to do, give your mentor a call—chances are, you'll be glad you did.

Bootstrap
Takeaways

Find a Mentor

1. Ask your mentor for feedback on how you're showing up as a leader.
2. Tap into your mentor's experience for insights about dealing with people or navigating the politics in your organization.
3. Don't make an important career decision without checking in with your mentors.

6

Just Like the CEO

Create a Personal Board of Directors

THERE'S A ROLE out there for you, a big one. You can do it in addition to your current job, too. It doesn't pay anything, but you will learn a lot. You get to work with people who care about you, and best of all, the subject matter is going to be something you're very interested in—you! What could be better than that?

Here's what you're going to do. First, think of yourself as the CEO of a company or the executive director of a nonprofit organization. There's no doubt that such top leaders have a tough job. But they do get a lot of help—and some of that comes from their built-in advisory group, the board of directors. The board is a fascinating concept; a group of experienced executives who come together a few times a year to advise and support the leader as he or she works to move the company forward. Although board members come in different shapes and sizes, they do have one thing in common: They all have a vested interest in seeing the top leader succeed. They contribute by offering honest feedback on strategy, advocating ethics and governance, and approving well-planned risk-taking and innovation.

Your own development as a leader has a lot of parallels to what the CEO or executive director is trying to accomplish. You're both looking to set a bold strategy (one of personal improvement). You're both striving for the highest ethical standards (in your leadership behaviors). Finally, you're both also setting a clear plan and taking a few risks to innovate (as you add new skills to your game). If you're doing this properly, you're working from a strategic plan, establishing a set of guiding principles that you won't compromise on, and taking some risks—just like the top leader. So why not borrow the board of directors' idea, too? Here's how to do it.

Select a Diverse Collection of Board Members

First, identify four to five people to serve on your PBD—your Personal Board of Directors. What are this group's members going to do? They're going to help you plan, execute, and assess your development as a leader. You're going to brief them on your plans and ask for their advice and suggestions. You're going to ask them to track your progress, give you feedback on how you're doing, and evaluate your results. In other words, you're going to set up a structure that ensures that you absolutely, positively achieve your development objectives. Unless, of course, you're willing to go to all this trouble and then NOT make an effort to improve. But you wouldn't do that, would you?

Start by choosing a PBD from among your peers, direct reports, extended team members, and matrix managers. Pick people who are familiar with your work, see you regularly throughout the year, and will give you a diverse set of opinions and suggestions. Don't choose your current boss (you get enough advice and feedback from him). The best combination depends on your development goals; if you're trying to be more patient and listen more effectively, choose two to three direct reports or people lower down in your group to be on the PBD. If you're trying to demonstrate more executive presence, lean toward a greater number of matrix managers (peers of your boss). The ideal composition is probably two peers, two direct reports, and one matrix manager. Because you want to meet with them in person, choose all of your PBD members from within your current organization (although it's tempting to "hire" your best friends or former colleagues for this assignment, don't do it. This is a job for people who see you every day). Obviously, once you've thought about who should serve on your PBD, you need to ask them if they'd be interested and gain their commitment.

Put Your Board of Directors to Work

And just what is this commitment? How does it work? Tell your PBD members that you'd like to meet with them as a group three times a year; each meeting should last about an hour. Schedule the first meeting right after your performance appraisal (if your company doesn't do performance appraisals, schedule the meeting when you're about to set your annual development objectives). Schedule the second meeting for six months later to check in on your progress. Schedule the third and final meeting just prior to the next performance appraisal cycle to collect final feedback on how you accomplished your learning goals during the previous year. Start the first meeting by thanking them for helping you focus on your development goals, and express your appreciation for signing on as your personal set of advisors. Share your development plan, and ask for their feedback and recommendations. Ask them to observe your behavior throughout the year in these areas, and invite them to provide constructive criticism and suggestions as they notice results or a lack of progress. Solicit recommendations in the very first meeting; find out what they think will or will not work as you pursue your goals. The second meeting is all about their feedback: What are they noticing? What are you doing well? What could you be doing even better? Finally, in the third meeting, gather even more input, and ask for suggestions on what you should tackle next in terms of personal improvement.

When I was promoted to my first vice president role, I used this technique because I really wanted to check myself against the standards and expectations of people at this level of the organization. I felt I needed regular, honest feedback about how I was showing up as an executive, so I asked a group of other VPs to serve as my PBD for the first year. Their recommendations were great, and their feedback helped me settle into my role. More important, they showed me how to truly be an executive. I'm still grateful for their guidance; it helped me get my feet on the ground after a stretch promotion.

At first, this might seem like a hokey idea; even your PBD members might find it a little strange. But after you meet a couple of times, it will feel pretty natural. All you're doing is asking a group of people—who already know you well and have a vested interest in seeing you succeed—to help you grow as a leader. This is something that you can do for yourself, no matter what size organization you work in. Just like the CEO or executive director uses the board to stress-test strategy and product ideas, you can use your Personal Board of Directors to evaluate your development as a leader. Try it—you'll find that there's nothing more motivating than publicly declaring your intentions to improve as a leader.

Bootstrap
Takeaways

Create a Personal Board of Directors

1. Identify a group of trusted colleagues to meet with you two to three times a year to discuss your development plan.
2. Expand the conversation by sharing your strategy or employee engagement plans with your PBD—solicit their reaction and feedback.
3. If this works for you, tell others about it; putting yourself out there is a great way to ensure you meet your commitments!

7

Get in the Weight Room

Identify and Leverage Your Strengths

YOU KNOW THE ADVICE pretty well by now. If you want to get in phenomenal physical shape, you have to cross-train and work on all aspects of your fitness. It's not enough to log five miles a day if you're a runner; you also should be lifting weights and stretching to keep your body at peak performance levels. The same is true of your leadership development "work out." If all you do is work on your developmental challenges, you'll ignore the biggest asset you have as a leader: your strengths. If you want to take your game to a new level, you have to identify and leverage what you do best. Think of your strengths as your core—you need to keep it strong because it enables everything else you do. Call it cross-training in reverse; while working on your weaknesses, don't forget to maximize your strengths.

Why is it so important to know and leverage your strengths? That's an easy question, according to Peter Drucker, the godfather of modern management study. In his 1999 *Harvard Business Review* article entitled "Managing Oneself," Drucker writes: "Most people think they know what they are good at; they are usually wrong. More often, people know what they are not good at—and even then more people are wrong than right. And yet, a person can perform only from strength. One cannot build performance on weaknesses, let alone on something one cannot do at all."[2] Drucker states the obvious in such eloquent terms: A person can perform only from strength. Makes sense, doesn't it? If all you had were weaknesses, you wouldn't be in a position to break out, move up, and take full advantage of your leadership skills.

So, it's clear that you need to get into the leadership "weight room" and build on your strengths. But what exactly are your strengths? What is it that you do really well? Identify your core strengths by answering the five basic questions presented below.

Be Honest with Yourself

Identifying your strengths only works if you're being absolutely honest with yourself. Although it's true that no one knows you better than you know yourself, sometimes we all have a tendency to mislead ourselves about our best qualities. But let's assume that you're going to do a thorough assessment of your own skills, and start with the first question: "What are my best qualities as a leader?" Another way to think about this question is to ask, "What am I most proud of?" Is it your calming presence? Your ability to influence the boss? Communicating to large groups? Creating a vision and strategy?

Answer the question of what really defines you as a leader. Write down your best qualities, with a brief description of each one. Keep the list brief by capturing your top four or five qualities (e.g., creativity, patience, optimism, integrity, collaboration). Once you've identified your best qualities, the trick is to leverage them as often as possible. For example, if developing people is one of your best qualities, how can you do even more mentoring or coaching across the organization? Take the time you're spending on unimportant tasks and spend that time teaching and nurturing emerging talent.

The second question is: "Which of my skills am I most confident in?" Think of skills as the building blocks for macro leadership qualities. What are your specific, go-to skills, and how do they enable you to achieve results? Are you good at creating presentations (which helps you articulate strategy)? Are you quick on your feet in front of an audience (which helps you as a communicator)? Break down your leadership into the component skills that enable you to demonstrate the right behaviors. The reason you're so good at influencing is not magical; it's a combination of specific skills. In this case, attention to detail, data analysis, interest in the industry, and political savvy. Get in touch with the skills you're most confident in. Just as you know if you're good at creating PowerPoint slides, you also know if planning, relationship building, and listening are among your most trusted skills. Once you define the specific skills (list your strongest six to eight), think about all the ways you could be combining these skills to maximize how you're showing up as a leader. For example, if relationship building and coaching are your strengths, should you be mired in daylong progress update meetings? Should you be leading a detail-oriented, data-driven task force project? Know your skills, and put yourself in position to accentuate them. Literally, assess each situation with this question: "Does this task make the best use of my skill set?"

The third question is: "In what situations am I really comfortable?" Is it staff meetings with your team? Brainstorming sessions with your peers? Meetings with the boss? Walking the halls or the shop floor? Being out on sales calls? Public speaking engagements? Knowing *where* you're at your best can be as important as knowing what you *do* best. Take the case of a musician who can play beautiful music—that's his skill. But maybe he's not at his best in all types of venues. Why is that? The skill hasn't changed but the environment has; maybe he's more comfortable with smaller audiences, or he doesn't like playing outdoors. The key is to know your Comfort Zones and leverage them. Try to control the environment in which you can do your very best work.

Next, ask yourself the fourth question: "What can I teach others?" What do you know so well that you'd have instant credibility as a teacher or mentor? What are you an expert at? Would you be comfortable building a learning curriculum around this knowledge, skill, or behavior? Chances are if you can't teach it, you don't know it well enough or haven't mastered it yourself.

Ask Others about Your Strengths

Don't just take your own word on this; it's important to also answer the fifth question: "What would others say are my strengths?" Ask your colleagues, particularly your boss, peers, and direct reports. You can do this in several ways, including a formal 360° feedback process (see Chapter 3) or an email campaign, but one of the easiest ways is just to ask them in a normal conversation. When you're having lunch or a one-to-one meeting, simply say: "I'm trying to identify what I do really well. What would you say my core strengths are?" Do this with six to eight colleagues to get a well-rounded sense of how others see you. Listen carefully, and thank them for their input. Hopefully, it fits with how you see yourself, but there may be a hidden strength or a blind spot that emerges from these conversations (see Figure 2).

Whatever your strengths, it's important to have a clear understanding of what they are and a plan for using them to drive results. We really do lead from our strengths; they form the basis for our daily actions and performance. As you focus on your developmental opportunities, don't forget to leverage what you do well, too. After all, your strengths have gotten you this far—keep building on them!

Bootstrap
Takeaways

Identify and Leverage Your Strengths

1. Make a list of your strengths—what you do really well. Be honest with yourself and hold a high bar for your definition of "strengths."

2. See your strengths through the eyes of others; ask for feedback about what you do exceptionally well.

3. Look for opportunities to leverage your strengths; put yourself in situations where you can make the most of your skills.

8

Go Back in Time

Ask Past Colleagues about
Your Leadership

MAKING YOURSELF INTO a more effective leader is hard work. You're not going to make all the right moves, all the time. Wait, we have established that you're not perfect, right? There is something you need to be working on, yes? Well guess what, that "something" has probably been there for a long time. Sorry to break it to you, but just as your leadership strengths are enduring, so too are your development opportunities. C'mon—you've always known about this weakness, right? Look back at the leadership journey you created in Chapter 1. If you're like most leaders, there are some persistent areas you still need to work on. Although you can learn new things and improve yourself as a leader, you're also remarkably consistent in your behavior patterns; change doesn't happen that easily. What is an opportunity for you today has probably never been the strongest part of your leadership game. It's OK to confront it. The first step in developing yourself is admitting that you have to break out and take charge of this, now.

Seek Out Former Colleagues

If you're serious about making a change, here's an interesting way of confronting the depth and extent of your development challenge.

Look back at your leadership history. You've probably managed quite a few people along the way; certainly, you've had a lot of peers and bosses. They all experienced your leadership a little differently, of course. What could you learn from them today if you called them up and asked for feedback about what it was like to work with you? How could their perspective (after having a few years to think about it) help you now? What stories could they tell that would still be true of your leadership style today? How hard can it be to call people from your past and ask them what you did well or could have done better?

Now before you say "there's no way I'm doing that," stop and think about this for a moment. This is an incredible opportunity. These are people that have experienced your leadership firsthand; people you impacted either positively or negatively (yikes—maybe this is scary!). Hopefully, they remember you fondly and benefited from your leadership. But who hasn't had a few bumpy relationships as a leader? The answer is we all have. And distance and time can sometimes bring much-needed maturity and perspective to what it was like to work with you. If you make an effort to collect input from people you used to lead, you can add a historical perspective to your current feedback. How great is that?

I've done this on two occasions, right after I took a new job. Knowing it was still fresh in their minds, I called the team I'd just left and asked for their feedback on my leadership. What I learned surprised me a bit; some of the things I was sure I had done right were not mentioned at all, and some of my concerns turned out to be nonissues. Because of the circumstances, I was also able to ask for specific feedback on how I could get off to a fast start with my new team; their ideas were great, and really helped me to be successful more quickly. I was definitely glad I asked for their input.

If you're willing to try this, seek out five people from your past to interview about your leadership. At least three of these interviews ought to be with people who worked directly for you;

peers or other colleagues can round out the feedback. Have these conversations in person or on the phone—don't do this via email. It may be that you haven't talked to some of these people in years; don't be intimidated by that! Yes, you might need to find them, set up the concept, and arrange the call. But if you've kept in touch with the people that helped you throughout your career, you should easily be able round up five people to call to have this conversation. Now, what do you ask them?

Ask Three Questions

The easiest way to complete this exercise is to keep it simple. First, tell them what you're doing, and ask them if they'll take this trip down memory lane with you. Be clear that you're trying to connect your past strengths and opportunities to how you're continuing to develop as a leader. If the past relationship was particularly good, prepare to be dazzled by your own leadership brilliance (be modest when accepting their endless praise). If you have the courage to call a former colleague where the relationship was a little rocky, start out by acknowledging that you know you weren't always the best manager. Show that you have at least some self-awareness about their experience working for you (this will set the tone that you're open to listening to their feedback, and it will keep them from hanging up before you even get started!).

Begin by asking: "When you worked for (or with) me, what did I do really well as a leader?" Focus them on your strengths first. Let them talk freely about your leadership style, but try to get specific about your core competencies—what specifically did you do that worked for them? Next, ask them: "What did I do that frustrated you or made your job harder?" In other words, ask, "Where could I have been more effective as a leader?" Asking where you fell short in this way makes it real for them. Rather than asking them to simply recall your weaknesses, you will be asking in a way that will stir some tangible memories and allow them to tell you what it really felt like when you weren't at your best (I know, you're freaking out again; but stay with this—be brave, you can do it!). Finally, ask this question: "Overall, what did you learn working for (or with) me?" Ask about your lasting impact—your leadership legacy. Good or bad, you probably made an impression in their lives and career; find out what it was. This can be the most profound (and rewarding) lesson you'll take away from this exercise. After all, although you may not be able to make a difference in their lives anymore, you certainly can impact your current and future employees. Get a sense of how your leadership shapes people long after you've stopped working with them.

If you really want to take stock of how far you've come as a leader, you need to take a trip back in time and check in with former colleagues. Reaching back into your past helps you identify consistent leadership strengths and opportunities and shines the light on your development progress. Hopefully, you still have all of the good leadership qualities they liked about you, and you've made significant strides in the areas that they remembered as weak. At the very least, you will have reconnected with some old friends and co-workers. Talking about what it was like to work for you, even years later, can be humbling and scary. It can also be incredibly productive and feel really good. No matter what you're expecting, you'll probably experience a little bit of both. Trust me, it's worth the effort.

Bootstrap
Takeaways

Ask Past Colleagues about Your Leadership

1. Ask former direct reports and peers what it was like to work with you. Tap into their perspectives, which have aged and matured with time.

2. Reach out to people you know enjoyed working for you as well as a few who struggled with your management. Get a balanced view of your leadership style.

3. Be humble, gracious, and appreciative. Thank them for their feedback, and weave it into your continuing efforts to improve your leadership skills.

9

Is There Another Way?

Confront Your Hardest-Held Positions

WHEN IT COMES to getting input on how you're showing up as a leader, you have two primary sources. The best source, of course, is other people who have experienced your leadership. This section of the book has included several techniques for collecting and internalizing that feedback, and you would do well to use them all to get a full picture of your strengths and opportunities. It may not be easy, but hey, it's only your career that's at stake, right? You need to do this—understanding how others see you is one of the best ways to take charge of your own development.

The second source of input might prove even more challenging because that source is you. Why is this so difficult? Because it's hard to be brutally honest about your own leadership skills. Just as most of us believe we're better drivers than we really are, most of us think we're better leaders than we actually are. However, if you've read the chapters in this section, you're well on your way to carrying out some serious self-reflection. Thus far, you've taken a hard look at your relationships and examined where you have an opportunity to improve your network (Chapter 2). Ideally, you were honest with yourself about where (and why) you need to work on certain relationships. You've also assessed your strengths to see what you can truly leverage to be a better leader (Chapter 7). Again, taking stock of your strengths involves being candid about what you do *really* well—reserve this category for those behaviors that truly stand out.

What Are You Absolutely Sure Of?

There's another self-reflection exercise that helps you assess your leadership brand, and this one might be the hardest yet. Make a list of your most rigid, hardened opinions or positions and see if there is something you can do about becoming more open and flexible. Take a long, constructive look at your most sharply drawn points of view, and see if they're still valid and useful. All of us have developed thought patterns over the years that guide our behaviors. Do you have any inflexible beliefs or attitudes? Are there any strong opinions that seem to be holding you back? Do you frequently get into debates or arguments about certain topics, where other people find you stubborn or closed off to reasonable conversations? For this to work, you need to be completely honest with yourself. Go find that magic mirror that gives you the real view of yourself—you'll need it for this exercise. The phrase "the truth will set you free" aptly applies here; if you can put your most strict beliefs on the table for consideration, anything's possible in terms of your growth as a leader.

Though the reason for this exercise may be obvious to some, it deserves elaboration. Great leaders consider all sides of an issue when setting strategy or making decisions. In a word, they're open-minded. They listen to different points of view and are willing to change their position if the facts are compelling enough. As a result, people generally love working for them, because they know their voices will be heard. Yes, the boss may make the final call, but when he or she is open to other ways of looking at things, others get a chance to take part in the discussion. As a leader, you have to develop the ability to listen to others' opinions, especially when they differ from yours, when considering a path of action.

You can't afford to be so resolute in your point of view that you're not willing to modify it; that's a leadership train wreck waiting to happen.

In my own career, there have been a few instances where my own stubbornness has gotten in the way of working effectively with others. One clear example comes to mind: It was a time when my inflexibility cost me precious leadership capital. For many years, I had a long-standing belief that executive assessments weren't appropriate for internal promotional candidates. My position, which I persistently defended, was that putting current executives through a formal assessment center was a poor substitute for the data we had accumulated on them to-date. In short, I felt promotions should be a by-product of the employee's track record at the company. To my detriment, I wouldn't budge from this point of view in discussions with my boss or other senior leaders. As a result, I lost some credibility as an expert and wasn't seen as a mature participant in this specific debate. My inability to see other possibilities or scenarios led to this discussion dying a slow death; we never did execute a formal assessment process for promotional candidates. Nevertheless, I still lost something. By holding on to my position with unwavering resolve, I cost myself a seat at future tables for these types of conversations and closed off an important avenue that my company might have otherwise explored. Why was I so stubborn? I can't fully explain it. I do know that it didn't make me look very professional, and I can appreciate now what I might have gained in the long run by being more flexible and open-minded.

So what's on your list of hardened positions? Do you have any rigid and inflexible beliefs? Are you "dug in" anywhere? As the leader, are you closing off discussions with your team because of your established opinions? Can you ever recall saying: "We tried that, it didn't work" or "We've always done it this way"? Maybe you've always had a bias against a particular tool or piece of software. Perhaps you harbor a personal view concerning your boss or a peer, which can be the most hardened position of all. In such cases, you may not consider others' points of view because you just can't bear to look at it from their perspective; there's no trust or respect left that allows that to happen. Or, maybe it's a philosophical issue; you simply feel a certain way and aren't willing to consider alternative positions. Be aware that these are dangerous corners to back yourself into; don't allow your own strict ideologies to close you off to new and different viewpoints.

Make the List Work for You

So, are there any positions you want to rethink before declaring yourself the world's expert? Try this exercise: Write "My Inflexible Positions" at the top left-hand side of the page and begin to fill them in, numbering them as you go. Don't stop writing until you've listed every hardened belief, attitude, and position you currently carry around in your head. Then, write "Other Possible Realities" at the top right-hand side of the page and list two or three alternatives for each of your inflexible positions. Get on the other side of the argument and write down other potential points of view.

When you're done, you'll have a nice roadmap for what you need to be open to in future discussions. You'll even have a head start to recognizing what the other positions look like. Then, watch your team's reaction the first time you say: "I'm open to discussing this; what are some other ways we could solve this issue?" Talk about a leadership transformation!

My advice to you is this: Don't be the leader who says, "You're not looking at this the right way." That's just intolerant; there are always multiple ways to look at things. Take an honest, objective view of your most unyielding positions at work, and see if you can't make a little space for a different way of thinking. In other words, widen the lens on how you look at the world; it's amazing what you can see when you let in more light. Your co-workers will definitely notice, and you'll probably enjoy the view.

Bootstrap
Takeaways

Confront Your Hardest-Held Positions

1. What positions or points of view do you carry around that are completely inflexible? Make a list of all your rigid opinions (and be honest!).

2. Now, what other points of view might be valid? Write down legitimate alternatives to your positions.

3. Open yourself to "possibility thinking." This is the art of looking at an issue from many different angles before settling on your point of view.

10

How Am I Driving?

Develop a Vision, Mission, and Strategy

IF YOU'VE TRIED THE IDEAS from the first nine chapters of the book, you've already started collecting feedback about your leadership behaviors and style. Good. Now you know how you're showing up as a leader. You've convened a Personal Board of Directors, found a mentor, and taken stock of your strengths. Check. You've been honest with yourself about your hardened opinions and even have a peer lined up to help monitor a specific development challenge. Excellent. You're doing everything you can to evaluate your leadership. There's just one more component to consider.

How are you at setting the *vision, mission,* and *strategy* for your group? Without question, setting compelling targets and stretch goals for your team is one of the most important of all leadership tasks. In fact, the higher up you go, the more critical it becomes. The leader must be able to motivate and focus people on these three elements; vision and mission provide purpose and direction, and strategy provides the roadmap for accomplishing your goals.

Now, you may get some input on these skills from peers and direct reports, but they don't always know what "good" looks like here. Your peers and direct reports typically will provide input on your listening skills, your meeting behavior, your ability to give and take feedback, your time management skills, your level of compassion, and so forth. However, it may be difficult to get clear feedback from direct reports and peers on your ability to visualize a dream and make it a reality. For this crucial dimension, it helps to get feedback from leaders higher in the organization, particularly executives who have experience developing vision and strategy.

To begin this journey, answer the following questions: 1) Have I clearly articulated *why* my team or department exists? 2) Is the team clear on *what* it is we're trying to accomplish? 3) Does everyone in my group know *how* we're going to accomplish our goals? If the answers to these questions are crystal clear, congratulations; you're a master at setting vision, mission, and strategy. If you're not quite sure of the answers, it's time to seek coaching and input from senior leaders. What follows is a look at each of the three elements of strategic planning and how to get a sense of whether you're on the right track.

Start by Establishing the Vision

The vision is the dream—the future state, where you want to go. Think of it as the *why*—as in, "Why does our group exist?" The vision should be aspirational and motivational, something the team can rally around. The vision describes the "big idea" or your long-term intentions, and it is fairly permanent. A couple of examples illustrate the grandness of the vision statement: Disney's vision is: "We create happiness by providing the finest in entertainment for people of all ages, everywhere." Levi's vision is: "We will clothe the world." Both of these aptly describe the ultimate vision these companies are trying to define for employees (and customers).

What's your vision statement? Why does your group exist? What are you striving for? If you haven't done so already, try crafting a vision statement for your team (it can be something that supports the larger company vision, for example). Simply get out a piece of paper and start writing. Or, if you feel comfortable doing so, work on this with your direct reports; it can be a great team exercise. Answer the "why are we here?" question. Aim high and make it aspirational. A great vision can unify a team and give its members a reason to come to work every morning.

Craft the Mission Statement

Once you define the vision, write a mission statement. The mission is the goal: the objective in front of you. Think of it as the *what*—as in: "What are we trying to accomplish?" The mission should be challenging and should describe the business you're in and the customers you're trying to serve (whether internal or external). The mission should be connected to the vision; that is, by accomplishing the mission, you move closer toward making the vision a reality. Also, missions can and do change; it's common for companies or groups to have different mission statements as the market ebbs and flows. Here are some examples of clear mission statements: Google's mission is to: "Organize the world's information and make it universally accessible and useful." Unilever's mission is to: "Add vitality to life, by meeting everyday needs for nutrition, hygiene and personal care with brands that help people look good, feel good and get more out of life." Both of these statements clearly articulate what employees should be focused on. The mission statement does just that; it provides the "true north" that guides employee performance; if your work does not support or drive the mission, then you are headed in the wrong direction.

Have you clarified your team's mission? Do all team members have a complete understanding of what they should be focused on? Again, drafting and socializing a mission statement is a great way to drive alignment around your primary objective—what you need to get done. Strive for simplicity and clarity, and make sure the mission statement is tied to the vision. Help your group make this connection; crafting the right "what" (mission) will help achieve the "why" (vision).

Develop the Strategy to Get There

Once you've crafted the vision and mission, the real work begins—developing the strategy. Think of strategy as the *"how"*—as in *"how are we going to complete the mission?"* Strategy describes the specific plans taken to meet the objective, and should be clear and measurable. Good strategy includes detail about how the work will be accomplished, and includes resources, responsibilities, budget, metrics, and milestones. At a company level, strategies will be required for multiple areas such as technology, customer service, sales, marketing, and pricing. At your level, it will be focused on how to accomplish *your* team's mission. Remember that strategy changes often; it's common for groups to have a one year strategy, and for people's performance objectives to align with the strategic plans.

What is your strategy? Can you articulate the macro plans you have in place this year to achieve the mission? Does everyone on your team know the strategy, and how they fit into the picture? You definitely need to get this right; aligning people to the strategy (and keeping them aligned) might be the most important leadership task of all. In fact, alignment around the strategy is so important that you should check in with your team a couple of times during the year to ensure everyone is still on board and that you're sharing accountability for making the strategy work (see Chapter 40).

Seek Feedback from Senior Leaders

As the leader, you need to take the lead in developing the vision, mission and strategy for your team or department; this is not something you can delegate. But you shouldn't do it alone— strategic planning is not a singular activity. Start by getting your thoughts together on the why, what, and how. Then, work with your team to flesh out the specifics of each element and strive to condense it to one page (see Figure 3 for a sample one-page strategy document). In addition, the "one-page philosophy" helps to keep your plan visible and alive. Tape it to your wall, post it in the conference room, or carry it with you to every meeting. Walk through it with your team members on a regular basis to remind them of the critical objectives, and tie everything you're doing back to this summary of your strategy. Remember, if your vision, mission, and strategy can't be articulated on a single page, it's probably too complicated.

Finally, when it comes to developing something as important as the vision, mission, and strategy for your group, you need to open up the process and let others weigh in. In this case, it's helpful to seek out the experts and get their advice and counsel. It's the best way to ensure a clear purpose, direction, and operating plan for your team. When you feel you have something to share, socialize it with some of your company's senior leaders. Seek out three leaders in particular: the head of your functional area (who will have good line of sight to how your strategy fits in with others in his or her department), a senior leader in Operations (who excels at looking at how the strategy can be "operationalized" to actually accomplish your mission), and a senior leader in the company who is known for being a good strategist. For this last source, seek recommendations; people definitely know who's good at creating strategy and will be able to point you in the right direction.

Seek additional input and ideas. Share your one-page strategy document and ask for feedback. What do senior leaders like about it? What's missing? What ideas do they have for improving the clarity or focus? Is it clear how you're going to measure effectiveness and productivity? These are experienced leaders, with a proven track record of setting strategy. Be a sponge in these meetings; soak up their wisdom, and add it to your final document. And then, don't hide the fact that you solicited input on your group's strategy; let your boss, peers, and team know that you sought and received feedback on your strategy from respected senior leaders. Not only will you expand your network and build relationships with these leaders, but you'll demonstrate your maturity and self-confidence by asking for their input.

Bootstrap
Takeaways

Develop a Vision, Mission, and Strategy

1. Spend time crafting the right vision, mission, and strategy for your team; this is your roadmap to success.
2. Involve the team in this exercise and pare it down on one page. Strive to share the document with everyone on your extended team.
3. Get advice from senior leaders—tap into their expertise, and get their help in developing a clear, purposeful strategic plan.

Part Two

Add Something New
to Your Game

IF YOU'RE SERIOUS about developing yourself as a leader, you
need to do more than just leverage your strengths and minimize
your weaknesses. Those are just the skills you have today. In order
to break out and move up the organizational ladder, you need to
continually add new elements to your leadership toolkit. The leaders who stand still are destined to stay at their current level or
even fall behind. If you're not constantly learning and adding
new capabilities, your peers will leave you in the dust, and you'll
be surpassed by the group of managers coming up behind you.
Don't think so? Better look around—those bright, ambitious
managers who thrive on development? They'd love to have your
job. In today's world, it's becoming clear that you have to expand
and improve your management skills if you want to grow with the
organization.

The first thing you need to do is figure out what leadership
means to you; it's hard to chart a new course of skills development
when you don't know the game you're supposed to be playing.
Moreover, you need to have a consistent way of talking about your
leadership philosophy. Is a concise articulation of who you are as

a leader in your repertoire? Do you have a specific plan for adding new skills, and in what areas do you need to focus? Where can you leverage a learning opportunity that also benefits the company?

Maybe you want to learn more about the origins of leadership and understand the foundational principles of managing people. Or maybe you're ready to pick up a business book that has nothing to do with your industry or function. Consider adding some new leadership techniques to your repertoire, such as coaching or a new way to empower your people. Why not create capacity for yourself by adapting some new time management skills? That would allow you time to actually think and reflect, which might lead to even more ideas for skills development. Now there's a worthy concept: more time to explore new ways to develop your leadership skills. You see how fun this is going to be?

11

Break Out the Dictionary

Craft Your Own Definition of Leadership

EVERY LEADER needs to be grounded in what leadership actually means. If you don't know how to define the very thing you're trying to do, how can you be successful at it? Seems obvious, but you'd be surprised by the number of leaders who don't know how to adequately explain leadership. When asked, "What does leadership mean to you?" many leaders are stumped; they're unable to offer a concise definition of the practice and art of leading others. Do you want to work for someone who can't define his or her role or purpose?

Being able to *define* leadership is a must if you're going to *demonstrate* great leadership. You need to be able to articulate what leadership means to you. When a junior team member asks you what leadership means, you need to be able to easily call up your answer—your elevator speech on leadership. Trust me, this is important. Down through the years, I've conducted about a thousand interviews with executives in all types of organizations, and I begin every conversation with this question: "What does leadership mean to you?" By my unofficial count, about two-thirds of the leaders I've interviewed have handled this question with ease and quickly shared their definitions of leadership. Many of them have been quite good, too. However, the other one-third of executives have struggled with this question, fumbling for words to describe what they spend their entire day doing. This might not be so alarming were it not for the rest of the story. In my work, I also talk to the people who report to these leaders. These conversations generally go one of two ways: either they describe their leaders as "the real deal—I love working for them" or they offer (with much frustration) the following observation, "they're clueless; they don't get it." Again, this is unscientific, but there appears to be a significant correlation between the leaders who can't articulate what leadership means and the "clueless" set. Ouch! Being able to share your definition of leadership seems to be one of the signs of a successful leader. This makes sense to me; if you're doing something all day, shouldn't you be able to describe it?

Crafting Your Definition of Leadership

There's an easy way to develop your own definition of leadership. Start by reading *The Leadership Machine* by Bob Eichinger and Michael Lombardo.[3] The authors present an impressive body of research that lists sixty-seven distinct leadership competencies, or traits, and contend that leaders must exhibit most (if not all) of these competencies when leading in today's organizations. On this list (or most any collection of leadership competencies), you'll find traits that will help you define what leadership means to you. Examples include: vision, strategic thinking, passion, courage, integrity, innovative, empowers others, customer focused, credibility, authenticity, optimism, and communication skills. These traits or skills are the building blocks of leadership.

Review a competency list and identify the traits that resonate with you. This is a different exercise than identifying your strengths (see Chapter 7). This is about articulating what you want to be known for as a leader. How do you want to be remembered? What do you want your legacy to be? Match this view of yourself to the competencies that best describe your desired leadership persona.

If you are demonstrating and leveraging the very leadership traits that you most want to be associated with, chances are you're "walking the talk," that is, your behaviors mirror your desired leadership traits. Here's my list of traits I believe a leader must have: credibility, vision, integrity, courage, passion, and optimism. This list helps me stay grounded in how I want to lead myself and others. Choosing your essential leadership competencies is a great way to get oriented with the language of leadership. Then, when someone asks you what makes a great leader, you have your list of competencies and can say: "I think a leader has to have. . . ."

Another way to describe leadership is to write a formal definition. The key to a well-written leadership definition is to represent the essence of your thoughts as concisely as possible. There are hundreds of leadership definitions on the Internet that you may access to see some examples. My own definition follows: *Leadership is about creating a vision that others want to be part of, creating a positive environment where great things can happen, and developing people to reach their full potential.*

Try crafting your own definition—it's fun, and you'll learn a lot about yourself in the process. Once you create your own definition of leadership, memorize it and use it often. Share it with your direct reports and their teams. If you have a large group, share it with all of your employees in an all-hands meeting. Become an evangelist for leadership, sharing your definition with others and inviting your colleagues to develop their own definitions. You need to do this exercise for yourself; no one else can tell you what leadership means. Don't be that leader who can't describe leadership; craft your definition to fit your own style and beliefs, and make it a regular part of your development and leadership conversations.

Bootstrap
Takeaways

Craft Your Own Definition of Leadership

1. Research leadership traits, or competencies, and identify the ones that mean the most to you.
2. Be known as a leader who has a point of view on leadership; be able to share your definition (what leadership means to you) at any time.
3. Study the great definitions of leadership; be a student of how others view the subject.

12

Put It in Writing

Prepare a Leadership Development Plan

THE FAMILIAR PHRASE, "What gets measured gets done" is an old
business mantra that means that when you set goals and hold
people accountable, work stands a better chance of getting accomplished. It also happens to represent the best way to add new
leadership skills. If you're really committed to development, you
should document your goals and objectives in a Leadership
Development Plan (LDP). The LDP is just what it sounds like: a
formal, written plan of the steps to take to develop yourself as a
leader. Typically, this one-page document lists your specific development objectives as well as the behaviors you're committed to
adding, enhancing, or stopping. If you want to hold *yourself* accountable for development, put your learning objectives in writing and share the LDP with your boss, your peers, and your team.
Tell them what you're working on; give them copies of the LDP
and ask them to hold you accountable for the behavior change.
Once you put yourself out there, you're committed—and that's a
good thing when you're developing yourself as a leader.

Create a Simple and Elegant LDP

Let's face it, most of us are apprehensive of change. Change is
often difficult, and it requires extra work. You have to adapt, make

adjustments; you have to *evolve*. Pulling yourself up by your own bootstraps involves change, and it isn't going to happen on its own. You must identify the changes you want to make and commit yourself to making them happen. The LDP is designed to help you meet both of these challenges (see Figure 4).

Start by articulating your overall leadership development goal at the top of the page. Make this goal aspirational, yet achieveable. This is the statement that best describes what you're trying to "turn yourself into" as a leader. Next, identify up to three critical development objectives and add these to the left column. These should reflect the major areas of improvement that you discovered throughout Part One of this book. Be sure to restrict yourself to no more than three things to work on at any one time; any more can be distracting and you won't make significant progress on any of them. Write clear objectives, using active verbs and specific language about what you intend to improve. The objectives should be so clear that your grandmother could understand what you're trying to work on (even if she doesn't really know what you do for a living!).

Plan for Attitude and Behavior Change

Next, for each development objective, record the specific thoughts or behaviors you want to add, enhance, or stop. Break your development plan down into two categories: attitude and behaviors. In the second column, capture any *attitude adjustments* you need to make to really drive progress in this area. Frankly, sometimes the root of the problem is a bad attitude or lack of intent. Your bad (or absent) behaviors may flow from how you feel about certain situations or people. For example, if you don't like your boss, chances are your outlook or attitude is what needs to be adjusted (e.g., accepting that you don't have to be friends, acknowledging that your boss is working a different agenda, admitting that maybe your boss is right, etc.). Maybe you panic about speaking in public; in that case, your fears are probably holding you back from making any behavioral progress. You get the idea. Write your "action items" as bullets, and try to document ways and ideas for *thinking* differently. Reach down for the good stuff here—don't be shy or reserved. If you know you really need to adjust your outlook in order to change, admit what you need to work on, and put it in writing. Because you will be sharing your LDP with others, write these clearly but carefully—use positive language that expresses your desired behavior. If your initial thought is, "Stop being defensive around the boss," you might instead write: "Keep an open mind when exchanging feedback with others." If an area of opportunity is to "get along better with my peers," write "look for opportunities to involve or engage my teammates on a regular basis." Think of these items as refining or adopting a new mindset; it's hard to execute new behaviors if you're still thinking about the situation or person in the same old way. Attitude and intent precede behavior—don't neglect this area of development.

Then move to the final column and document what you really want to start *doing* differently. Strive to identify behaviors that others are sure to notice (these might include demonstrating new skills, increasing the things you do well, eliminating bad habits, etc.). These items should be mini action plans; they should describe measurable behaviors. Be very descriptive (and prescriptive). For example, if your development objective involves being completely present in meetings, one of your behaviors might be: "Leave my BlackBerry in the office when attending my team's staff meeting." This is a behavior change that others will certainly notice. In fact, your peers, direct reports, or manager should be able to easily recognize what you're working on and track your progress against each one of these items. For both the attitude and behavior columns, think quality, not quantity. For each development objective, record no more than two to four actionable items per column.

Finally, at the bottom of your LDP, document your key behavior enablers. This is a handy way to remember the two or three critical behaviors that drive everything on the page. For example, "getting out of my office" is an enabling behavior that can jump-start several different development opportunities, such as spending more time with your team, listening more effectively, learning about the business, spending time with internal clients, and so forth. You might repeat items you captured above; that's OK. The key behavior enablers are the absolute "must-dos" of your Leadership Development Plan.

For the past several years, I have created an LDP in late December for the coming year. I find that I'm in a reflective mood around the holidays, and I enjoy the process of documenting my learning and development objectives for the new year. Sometimes I even use the dual categories of attitude and behaviors to make adjustments in my personal life, and I often find my most successful development happens when I set challenging goals for myself in the attitude column (attitude really does set up behavior; it's all part of the ongoing maturation process).

If it's true that what gets measured gets done, then adapt that phrase for your development and say: "What gets *documented* gets done." Are you serious about working on your leadership skills? Well, here's your chance to write it down and share it with the world. Of course, you still have to execute the plan. But if you put in the time to create a robust development plan, you will have a terrific roadmap and monitoring tool as you make the commitment to change.

Bootstrap
Takeaways

Prepare a Leadership Development Plan

1. Document your plans for development and change.
2. Be bold—strive to create plans that you'll execute. Use the LDP to stretch yourself.
3. Share your LDP with others—don't be shy. Others need to know what you're working on in order to support you, and you'll be more likely to succeed if you put yourself out there.

13

One Year at a Time

Develop One Leadership Skill a Year

WHEN IT COMES TO LEADERSHIP development, how big are you willing to dream? Can you handle something on a grand scale—what might be the ultimate leadership development plan? Are you up for an extended affair with a particular leadership skill? Let's face it: When it comes to formal classroom development, it's hard to keep your skills polished after the course is over. Even if you attend a weeklong university program, there's a good chance the knowledge gained will fade over time. It can also be a challenge to apply what you're learning back on the job. So how about a development journey so comprehensive and relevant that it will permanently change your skill level? Would that get your attention? If so, welcome to the one-skill-a-year learning experience. That's right—a significant focus on one skill for an entire year.

Think about this concept: Develop one skill or behavior per year. It's not as radical as you might imagine. Let's say you're the average leader who begins managing people sometime in your late twenties. Let's also say you're likely to have a thirty-year career. Even if you worked on just one skill a year, with this plan you'd master at least a dozen top leadership behaviors before your fortieth birthday, just when you're hitting your stride as a leader. Would you be interested in having world-class skills in that many facets of leadership? Now you might be thinking: "I can't wait that long to develop my leadership skills—I need to get better at a whole lot of this stuff right now." OK, I like your attitude, but you need to be realistic. You can't even try out all the ideas in this book at once, let alone create formal learning plans for a dozen or more skills at the same time. But if you focus your efforts and set a goal of learning everything you can about one leadership skill, just think of what you could accomplish with twelve months of focus! Here's how to do it.

Pick a Specific Leadership Behavior

The first thing to do is choose the leadership area you want to work on. I recommend you think beyond the normal list of leadership competencies or traits, and select a full-blown leadership behavior. Leadership behaviors are actions you take on a daily basis, and each one requires a collection of various competencies. Think of leadership behaviors as "macro" actions that are enabled by "micro" competencies. For example, "building high performance teams" is a leadership behavior that is made up of a host of competencies, such as evaluating talent, setting goals, creating vision and strategy, resolving conflict, motivating and empowering others, etc. Share your plan to work on a single leadership behavior for an entire year with as many people as you can, and gather their input and advice. Consult your latest 360° feedback report (see Chapter 3) and determine where such a focused effort can make the biggest difference for you—both now and in the future. After all, this skill is going to stick with you, so be strategic about how you're going to add this deep level of expertise.

For illustrative purposes, let's pick "Driving Innovation" as the target leadership behavior, and let's plot a twelve-month plan that has you moving through three integrated learning phases: *study*, *practice*, and *teach*. In the first quarter of the year, you're going to study the topic by reading books, surfing the Internet, and consulting experts inside and outside your company to learn everything you can about innovation. Spend time in early January getting ready for your learning blitz by lining up your resources, buying three or four books on the subject, bookmarking Web sites, finding a conference to attend, identifying local companies known for innovation, etc. Next, organize all of your resources and planned trips and schedule them on the calendar; carve out time every week from January to March to spend time with your favorite research topic. Then, execute the plan. Yes, this means actually reading the books, calling the companies to arrange visits (see Chapter 29), and attending that conference in Phoenix in late March.

By the time April rolls around, you're going to know everything there is to know about driving innovation, and you'll probably have a few ideas that no one's thought of yet. Now it's time for the next phase: practice. Dedicate the next two quarters to applying what you've learned on the job. Set up an innovation lab in your department or division. Set a goal of brainstorming product or process innovations with your team. Volunteer to lead a task force that is looking at new ways to innovate. Write a white paper about the history of innovation in your company. Ask to meet with senior leaders to make a presentation about innovation, and make a pitch about where the company has the best opportunities for a new breakthrough. In other words, make a concentrated effort to lead innovation; make it part of your DNA for the next six months. It is important to make a plan and set goals—don't simply tell yourself that you'll play around with this concept. Figure out what you're going to do, and then do it.

Finally, in the last three months of the year, move into the teaching phase. Volunteer to teach a course on innovation at the corporate university or organize and market a speaker series where you travel around the company and make presentations about innovation (see Chapter 34). If such opportunities are not available within your organization, consider teaching a course on innovation at a local community college. What's the point of this phase? If you've ever taught a course, you already know; when you have to teach something, you really have to learn it. Knowing that you'll be in this phase at the end of the year serves to motivate you to strongly focus on knowledge gathering in the first three months (so you know *what* to teach). Likewise, if you know you're going to teach the subject, you'll document all those rich stories during the summer, so you can load up the course with real examples. Make an outline of your learning objectives, and do a dry-run with your team. Once you've completed your teaching commitment, take the last couple of weeks of the year off, or use them to prepare a development plan for another leadership behavior starting in January.

What do you think? Can you do it? A full year of development is ambitious, no doubt. It requires a lot of dedication and perseverance. But if you are able to do this with your weakest leadership skills over a six- to eight-year period, your proficiency will markedly increase—without question, you can turn those opportunity areas into towering strengths. Give this plan some thought the next time you find yourself frustrated over the lack of improvement of a particular leadership skill or behavior. Maybe all you need is the time and focus to do it right.

Bootstrap
Takeaways

Develop One Leadership Skill a Year

1. Pick out one leadership behavior each year to become really proficient at; become an expert in this area.

2. Study the theory and best practices of this behavior, and practice relentlessly to improve your skills during the year.

3. Learn this behavior so well that you can teach it to others by the end of the year; teach a class to share your expertise.

14

What Is It That Only You Can Do?

Learn to Delegate

HAVE YOU BEEN PROMOTED recently? Maybe into a new supervisory position or a step up the ladder into senior management? If so, congratulations and good luck; you're probably busy learning the ropes at the next level. Just don't forget the secret of moving on up. You know—the secret to maintaining your sanity and actually having a life; the key to being wildly productive and successful; the one management technique that you really have to master as you move higher in the organization.

What, they didn't tell you this when they promoted you? That's OK; I'm going to share it with you right now. The secret to being effective at the next level of leadership is delegation. Now, I know what you may be thinking: That's it? Delegation? You bet it is. When you move to a higher level, you have to lead differently; you can't do all the work anymore. That may have worked in your last position. But up here, you'll get buried in a heartbeat if you don't learn how to leverage your team effectively. You have more resources now—learning to use them is the secret to making your mark in this new role.

Become a Master of the What, Not the How

Delegation is the act of committing and entrusting an assignment or task to someone else. It also involves transferring power and authority. This last point is critically important, because delegation isn't micromanagement. In fact, it's the opposite. When you delegate something, make sure to allow the employee to add his or her personal touch to the project or assignment. Yes, you can outline the basic parameters, but let the person do it his or her own way. As a leader, you should become known as a "master of the what, not the how." Focus on developing the big picture; let your people fill in the painting with their own imagination and creativity.

Effectively allocating work to others requires that you pay attention to three primary factors: the *why, what,* and *who* of delegation. First, *why* do you want to become adept at delegating? There are many reasons, but here are the four primary ones: 1) Delegating increases work output. By putting the right work in the hands of the right people, you maximize your team's productivity. 2) Delegating fosters growth and development. When you put your team in a position to learn new tasks, they gain knowledge and develop skills. 3) Delegating keeps employees motivated and engaged. People want to be involved; they don't want to be micromanaged or spend all of their time on menial tasks. 4) Delegating allows you to focus on high-level work. It frees you to concentrate on your most important tasks—the stuff that only you can do.

Now that you know why you should be delegating work, you need to know *what* to delegate. Although there's no exact list of what you should and shouldn't delegate, a general rule of thumb is that you should consider delegating *anything* that someone else can do, and *nothing* that only you can do. In other words, keep work that only the leader can do, tasks such as setting strategy, coaching, developing the team, solving critical performance or conflict issues on your team, being in meetings where your presence is required, and so forth. However, if a task is not something that only you can do, delegate it to someone else.

Delegation took me awhile to learn, frankly. Like most leaders, I moved up the ranks because I was good at what I did—and when I first moved to a higher level, I thought I needed to do even more of what I had been doing. I quickly found out that wasn't going to work; there were a whole new set of challenges waiting for me, and I couldn't do everything myself anymore. To succeed, I *had* to learn to delegate. I started slowly, giving away my presentation and report writing first; I removed myself from the creative process and instead adopted a final reviewer role. Next, I gave away responsibility for meeting with vendors and making purchasing decisions—my people knew the hardware and software better than I did anyway. Finally, I began to give away meeting oversight and let my direct reports rotate in the role of planning and organizing our staff meetings. It was hard at first, I'll admit; I felt I was losing control. Eventually though, I benefited greatly—I literally gained ten to twelve hours a week to focus on more important tasks. You can do this, too. Examples of work you definitely should delegate are administrative tasks, report writing, presentation preparation, and budget analysis. As new work comes your way, ask yourself, "Is this something that only I can do?" If the answer is no, starting thinking of who you can ask to take on the assignment.

How do you know *who* to choose for an assignment? When the work is flowing in, you may have choices as to where it should be delegated. You might be tempted to keep loading up your star player—but that's a mistake. Spread the work around; get everyone involved. In fact, you might keep a delegation log or diary to keep track of who's been assigned what. As the tasks come in, consider these four factors when determining who should get the assignment:

1. **Their experience, knowledge and skills.** What knowledge, skills, and attitude do your people already have? Who needs what for continued development? Do you have the time and resources to provide necessary training? Is there time to redo the job if it's not done properly the first time?
2. **Their exposure to senior management.** Who needs more face time with your boss? Who do you want to showcase? What are the consequences of not finishing the project on time? How important is it that the work is done with the highest possible quality?
3. **Their preferred work style.** How independent are your people? How do they handle unexpected work falling into their laps? What do they want from their jobs? What are their long-term goals and interests, and how do these align with the work proposed?
4. **Their current workload.** Who has capacity? Does anyone have the time to take on more work? Will the delegation of this task require reshuffling of other responsibilities and workloads? Is this a task that will be recurring in the future?

Once you've delegated the task, don't forget to check in once in awhile to gauge progress. It's important to monitor performance and be available for questions and any other needs. Oh, and remember to give your people feedback during and after the project.

Congratulations again on that promotion. Enjoy the ride; you've earned this new leadership role. And what about all those people that report to you? Use them! Put them to work in creative ways and help them pull themselves up by their own bootstraps, too. Leaders differ widely in their ability to delegate with grace and style, but it is something you can get better at through experience. If you want to improve this aspect of your leadership brand—if you want to be known as a master of the what, not the how—start delegating.

Bootstrap
Takeaways

Learn to Delegate

1. Delegation is your most precious management resource. It allows you to get more work done and frees you up to focus on critical tasks.
2. Get good at delegating—now. You won't survive doing everything yourself; start getting the team involved.
3. Once you delegate, step back. You're giving others the assignment, and also the authority to do it their way. They may not do it exactly as you would, but that's OK—they might do it better!

15

The Whistle and the Clipboard

Practice Your Coaching Skills

THERE'S ONE LEADERSHIP SKILL that will set you apart from other leaders—and the good news is that you can master it if you're willing to apply some discipline and patience. While some leadership skills are must-haves that serve as antes into the game, other skills are icing on the cake that put you in a completely different category. Examples of must-have skills include strategic thinking, communications, delegation, and drive for results. If you lack these skills, you won't ever get to the top of the organization. But even the most senior leaders are sometimes lacking the one skill that can take you to a whole new level: coaching.

It's often said that "great leaders are known for the questions they ask, not the answers they give." Asking questions has to do with seeing the future and pushing the organization forward, but it also applies to coaching. Coaching is all about asking questions; it's about facilitating reflection and the search for answers. It's not about giving the answers; in fact, too many managers build an empire where every decision has to go through them. This is the antithesis of coaching. Coaching is about helping others solve their own problems and find their own answers. Great leaders know how and when to coach, and you can learn too, no matter your level in the organization. But it takes diligence and practice. You can be taught the basics, but you'll have to make yourself into a good coach through repetition and attentiveness. No one can do it for you; you must be committed to this approach to leadership if you want to be known for your coaching style.

A Different Kind of Impact

Do you remember the impact of your childhood coaches? Chances are you played sports or pursued a creative challenge such as dance, music, art, etc. Think of the best coaches you ever had and recall what a huge influence they had on you. Their impact was far greater than just the sport or activity you were engaged in. They taught you life lessons, boosted your overall confidence, and served as inspirational role models. They shared their wisdom, yes, but also encouraged you to find your own ways of taking your game to another level. That's the kind of reputation *you* can have if you master the art of coaching.

Let's start by contrasting coaching to mentoring (see Chapter 5). In essence, mentors provide answers; they share their point of view, offer solutions, and give advice. You seek out mentors to learn from their experiences. Coaches ask questions; they strive to get the individual to see possibilities, explore alternatives, and reflect on their own thoughts and behaviors. Coaching is a purposeful conversation where the goal is to unlock insight and awareness. As a leader, you can both mentor and coach, of course, sometimes even in the same conversation. But oftentimes, it's appropriate to move entirely into coaching mode with a direct report, a peer, or even your boss. Sometimes you want to do nothing but ask questions to help the person find their own solutions.

Three Fundamental Skills

There are three fundamental skills you'll need to be a good coach. First, you have to be a good *listener*. That means you must have the patience to let the other person talk without dominating the conversation. In fact, if you're doing this right, you're doing very little talking at all. Second, you have to be *focused*. You can't be distracted, stressed, or preoccupied. In order to keep the conversation moving and find the next line of questioning, you have to pay attention and be immersed in it. Finally, you must have *empathy*. You need to have the capacity to imagine what it's like to be in the other person's position. The ability to empathize is critical to the coaching process, as it not only helps you accept the other person on their own terms but also helps you to tune in to emotions and feelings that they themselves might not even be fully aware of. If you can bring focus, empathy, and the ability to listen to a solutions-oriented conversation, you can make that interaction a coaching opportunity. So how do you effectively use coaching as a management technique? Following are the basic elements of a productive coaching conversation.

The Coaching Process

A simple three-step coaching process always keeps me on track when I coach executives. Step one begins with getting the story. Simply ask: "What's on your mind today?" or "What's your biggest challenge right now?" Start by letting the individual share what the issues are—in other words, get the facts; establish the *what*. Continue until you have a firm grasp of the circumstances the person wants to discuss. Essentially, you're listening to the past—events that have already occurred. Next, move the person to the present and find out how he or she currently feels about the situation. What are this person's emotions, beliefs, feelings? How is he or she reacting to or behaving in light of this situation? What impact is it having on this person's psyche or performance? Ask a lot of probing questions here; one useful technique is to ask why five times to get to the root of a person's emotions. Do not skip this critical step. You need to understand how this individual is processing the event, that is, how he or she views it (for example, this person may not be taking accountability for his or her portion of the issue).

Finally, lead the individual into the future—the land of solutions and attitude or behavior change. Ask several questions designed to stimulate ideas for alternatives, resolutions, and so forth. It's OK to offer suggestions about solutions someone might *consider*, but resist the urge to tell the individual what to do. Coaching works best when the individual formulates his or her own answers. In the end, it's about individuals changing their perceptions, attitudes, and mindset—and you can't do that for them.

I have been coaching leaders for a long time and have found that this simple approach of getting the story, probing for feelings, and gently guiding clients to the solutions phase works most of the time. When I'm at my best, I understand the situation so well that I feel as though I'm actually in the story. When I fully understand the story, I gain the full measure of how they're feeling about the issues—maybe even beyond what they have admitted to themselves. When I really know how they feel, I can guide them to an appreciation for solutions and change, so they can't wait to try out new behaviors. When coaching works, the result is magical; your direct reports or peers will feel like they've made significant progress on their issue, and you'll have the satisfaction of helping them with a skilled and compassionate approach.

Oh, and one last thing. Although asking questions can be a terrific way of interacting with people in short bursts, if you're going to really use coaching as a management tool, you need to create the right environment. Set aside ample time for the discussion (at least thirty to forty-five minutes), meet somewhere in private, and position yourselves in a collaborative manner (lose the desk). It also helps to declare that you're going to be asking questions, essentially "asking permission" to move into a coaching mode for this conversation. This is especially important if this isn't your normal style of interaction. In brief, make sure the individual is comfortable and that you have plenty of time for a meaningful conversation.

You can do this—you can add coaching to your leadership toolkit. If you're serious about this, read a book or enroll in a course on coaching so you can learn additional techniques and skills from experts. And then practice your coaching style; find the right opportunities to use your new skills to help someone resolve an important issue. You won't be perfect right away, so monitor your own performance as you build the skills. Keep track of how many times you interrupt, offer advice, or fail to ask open-ended questions. Over time, you'll improve, and it will seem more natural to conduct conversations in this style.

If you're searching for the keys to a great leadership legacy, coaching can be a big part of your reputation. People may not always remember what you did as a leader, but they'll certainly remember what it felt like to work for you. If you demonstrate concern and interest for people, listen empathetically to their issues, and help them find their own way, they won't forget you. In fact, your coaching style will probably be imprinted on them, thereby ensuring that the approach will be paid forward to future generations. You want to add something new to your game? Become a better coach. In the end, it might just be the most fun you'll ever have as a leader; I'm almost certain it will be the most rewarding.

Bootstrap
Takeaways

Practice Your Coaching Skills

1. Add coaching to your leadership toolkit and start practicing your listening, focusing, and empathy skills.
2. Don't try this without conviction; you need to *want* to adopt coaching as a leadership technique for the right reasons.
3. Coaching is an art that you can continuously perfect. Be self-critical, and reflect on what you're doing well and what you can improve, and then make adjustments to your approach.

16

Hit the Books

Read Three Business Titles a Year

"PSSSST! HEY FELLA, over here—on your bookshelf. Yeah, I'm talking to you, Mr. or Ms. Leader. You bought me a year ago and stuck me next to this stupid binder that hasn't seen the light of day in ten years. Is that my fate? Are you ever going to read me? What'd you buy me for, anyway? You know, I could have gone home with that hard-charging manager down the hall who would have put me to good use. Maybe I would have been loaned out to other people, so my knowledge and ideas would flow around the company. But noooo, you're too busy to read me. Did you buy me just to fill up this bookcase and make yourself look smart?"

If your books could talk, would any of them say this to you? Are you buying the latest business and leadership books and actually reading them, or are you just doing the buying part? It's OK to admit that you're behind in your book reading; at least you're buying the books with the best intentions. Some leaders don't invest in business books. They don't have the time, and they don't see the value, which is a shame, because there are several benefits to staying current with a regular reading strategy. Because you're reading this right now, you've already demonstrated the willingness to pick up *and* read a book (by the way, thank you for picking this particular book). Here are three reasons to keep on reading.

Hit the Books

Three Reasons Why Business Books Matter

All of us lead busy lives and admittedly it's hard to find the time to read the average 250-page business book. With so many demands for our reading time—between the newspaper, business magazines, trade journals, and the Internet, not to mention reports, presentations and white papers at work—who has the time to read an entire business book? Another downside to investing time in business books is that many could be condensed into twelve-page articles that capture just the key points. OK, those are the argument against business books: no time, and they're too long. Fair enough. Now here are three reasons why you can't afford NOT to read them.

First, a lot of big, new ideas are hatched in business books. For example, *In Search of Excellence* sparked the whole reengineering movement.[4] The fact is, as a leader, you just can't afford to overlook classic or best-selling books; you need to read them to stay competitive and to be credible and current with your team and colleagues. Oh sure, you can take your chances at the next senior staff meeting when they're talking about *The World Is Flat* or *The Tipping Point*.[5] Go ahead, respond with: "I've never heard of that book—what's it about?" if you like, but you do so at your own peril.

Second, the business book captures one of the lost arts of leadership: storytelling (for more on the power of storytelling, see Chapter 19). Books have the space to tell multiple stories through real-life examples and parables. In fact, the "business book as a parable" format is alive and well (see *Our Iceberg Is Melting* or *The Five Dysfunctions of a Team*).[6] Business books expose you to the magic of storytelling and are a rich source of powerful stories that you can add to your own portfolio. Leaders such as Andy Grove (*Only the Paranoid Survive*), Lou Gerstner (*Who Says Elephants Can't Dance*), Bill Gates (*The Road Ahead*), and Jack Welch (*Winning*) share dozens of stories in their books.[7] Reading them has a cumulative impact on you as a leader—you learn *how* to tell stories, and you take away the essence of their examples to use in your own story.

Third, the business book is a vehicle for provocation and a driver of innovation. The business book makes you think precisely because you invest so much time in it. Read an eight-page article and you probably forget its contents a week later. But read a business book over the course of four to six weeks, and its message stays with you. The difference is that you must interact with a business book—you have to pick it up and put it down multiple times, and all the while, you think about the concepts, assertions, data, and ideas. Reading a business book over the course of a month allows you time to fully digest its concepts and incorporate them into your own business strategies and challenges.

Making the Business Book Work for You

Here are some of my tricks for making the business or leadership book a regular part of my development routine. First, I make an annual commitment to a read a specific number of business books per year: I put it in my development plan and try to stick with it. Second, I pick out the books ahead of time and put them in a high traffic zone at home—someplace where I'll see them often (face it, you're not going to read a book at work; you won't have the time, and if you do, it may mistakenly appear like you have nothing better to do). Third, I pick out the books myself. Most people buy a business book because it was recommended to them; they don't even know what it's really about when they order it. Go down to the bookstore and look for something that catches your eye (one effective technique is to buy three new books on your birthday every year; then set a goal of reading them by your next birthday). Try picking one book on leadership, one that relates to your functional area or expertise, and one that approaches a traditional business problem in a new way (i.e., *The World Is Flat*).

I generally read about eight books a year, with a plan of reading one or two chapters a week for a month. I don't try to read the whole book in a single weekend; instead, I make plans up front to "eat the book in small bites." In the past, I've also invested in books on CD and have downloaded books to my iPod for mobile listening. I've made room for the business book in my regular routine of keeping up-to-date on what's happening in the world, and it's always worked for me. I encourage you to add the same discipline to your ongoing development strategy. Be a trendsetter by picking up on a new book early—it's doubtful that the guy down the hall is reading it. Not only will you benefit from its ideas but also it will demonstrate to your boss that you're on the cutting edge.

The bottom line is that leaders need to read. It's part of your job to stay current, to find new ideas, to challenge the status quo. When visiting senior leaders throughout the organization, peruse their bookshelves to find out what they're reading. Ask your customers or business partners what they're reading, and see if it has implications for your business. Ask your team to read a particular book, and debrief the book together during one of your staff meetings. Don't be one of those leaders who says with pride: "I don't read business books." Frankly, that's just ignorant, and not very impressive. Commit (or recommit) yourself to reading a few good business books a year, including the one you bought last year that is just waiting to get off your office bookshelf and go home in your briefcase.

Bootstrap
Takeaways

Read Three Business Titles a Year

1. Reading hasn't gone out of style; as a leader, you need to stay current on the latest business thinking. Pull a few of those unread books off your shelf and start reading.

2. Challenge your team to read a book together—everyone takes a chapter and leads the weekly or monthly debrief.

3. Start with a goal of reading just three books a year. Read each one a chapter at a time over six weeks. Budget time in your schedule to read—you can do it.

17

The Best Thinking Tools
Ever Invented

Keep a Journal

HAVE YOU WRITTEN the great American novel yet? Well, maybe that's too ambitious; let's bring it down a level. How about an article for a magazine or trade journal? Not enough time, got it. What about a blog on the company Web site? No? Hmm . . . how about a letter to your parents? What? OK, I get it; you don't write anymore—at least not in the traditional sense. I know you type on a computer keyboard; you probably write 100 emails a day in addition to PowerPoint presentations, Word documents, and so forth. Maybe you crank out proposals, spreadsheets and production charts too—tools of the modern trade. But chances are you're not doing a whole lot of writing with pen and paper. That's too bad, because a lot of self development can flow out of your pen. To capture this value, I encourage you to add another skill to your leadership toolkit: the act of journaling.

When's the last time you sat down and did a little reflecting using the two greatest thinking tools ever invented? That's right, a little "pen and paper time" focused on your own thoughts can go a long way to recharging your batteries and helping you see things more clearly. Journaling is becoming a lost art. Not even thirty years ago, it was fairly common for children to keep diaries and for managers to keep journals—both filled with hopes, dreams, ideas, reflections, etc. Today, it seems we're too busy to pause and write down our thoughts and feelings. That's unfortunate, because writing can be therapeutic; there's something about it that slows the mind and causes a person to think. Keeping a journal is one of the last best personal reflection tools left in our world; it's something that only you do and only you see. It's a way to give your inner voice some time and attention. By committing your thoughts to paper, you give them credibility and validation.

I always encourage my executive coaching clients to keep a journal because it has a way of focusing them on the things that matter. Some of them embrace it, and some of them resist it, and not everyone gets the hang of it. However, many of my clients find that it helps them identify what's really important in their lives, both at work and at home. Writing your thoughts down on paper is a good way to remember and act on them.

Three Ways to Keep a Journal

Right about now you might be thinking: "No thanks; I've tried that; it's not for me." Well, that may be so, but there are many different ways to keep a journal, and you probably haven't tried them all. Here are three forms of journaling; try to make one of these a part of your regular routine. First, of course, is the old standby: the longhand, free-flowing diary. This version has an added bonus: You get to buy a really nice leather-bound journal! Seriously, this can be half the fun; go to an office-supply store and let your creative side run wild through the journal/notebook section. Pick out something that appeals to you, something you'd carry around with you or leave out on your desk at work. The longhand journal has a long and storied tradition, of course, that dates back thousands of years. Open the book and start writing. If you want to track your thoughts sequentially, date the entries. Otherwise, let your imagination go—there's no limit to your direction here. Draw pictures, use different colored pens, write big or small or sideways on the page. Write it in the first or third person—it doesn't matter. This is your canvas; paint on it as you wish. Keeping a diary-style journal allows you to constructively daydream about your role, your team, how you're showing up as leader, and so forth. It's like taking your mind and imagination to a fancy spa: Using this technique regularly can be incredibly energizing.

The second journaling technique is more of a note-taking process. It involves keeping a designated notebook with you at all times—one you leave open on your desk, take to meetings, etc. This technique allows you to write down all the random thoughts that come to you during the day or in a meeting in four major categories. Write the date on a piece of paper, and divide the page into four equal quadrants.

Label the upper left quadrant "Learnings," and use it to capture new information, facts, or figures that you read or learn during the course of your day. Use this space to record anything that you want to remember to tell your team, for instance. What resonated with you today? What did you learn? Write it down.

Label the upper right quadrant "Ideas," and use it to jot down any new ideas that this new information creates for you. Write down the *implications* of what you learned; anything that has application back to your team. This can be an exciting set of notes, as new ideas pop into your head, sparked by what you learn. In other words, make this a series of bullets about how you might apply what you've learned back on the job.

Label the lower left quadrant "Questions," and use it to write questions your want to explore back on the job. For me, these questions often start with: "What if we?" or "Can we?" or "Should I?" Let your mind wander a bit; these questions may or may not be associated with what you're currently reading or listening to, but once you get on a roll, you can fill a sheet of paper with just basic questions you want to find the answers to—either by yourself or as a team.

Finally, label the lower right quadrant "Reflections," and use this space to capture self-reflections about your leadership. Jot down two or three things you've been doing really well as a leader lately, and a few things you know you should be working on. Write down ideas for behavior change as you push yourself to improve as a leader.

The third and final version of the journal technique involves keeping detailed notes about each of your direct reports. Using a folder or a binder with tabs, create a section for each direct report. Then, in your one-on-one or staff meetings, record clear and consistent notes about the following topics:

- Delegation. What tasks have you delegated to them?
- Progress. What do you want to follow up on?
- Accomplishments. What have they done that you want to praise and remember?
- The Real Life. Who's important to them? What's going on in their world?
- Career Aspirations. What are their hopes and dreams? How can you help?
- Fun Facts. What's their favorite candy? Musical artist?

This is an easy way to stay connected to your direct reports, and because it's in the book you always carry with you, you're never far from a quick review of what you talked about last time, what you want to follow up on, what's important to them, and so on (for more on getting to know your direct reports, see Chapter 25).

The next time you're feeling overwhelmed or unorganized, take out your journal and start writing. Make self-reflection a real habit. It's a routine that has residual value; because it's down on paper, you can go back and read your notes any time. Challenge yourself to make journaling an everyday practice; it helps you to keep track of all those random thoughts. And who knows, you might develop a love of writing that will lead directly to that best-selling novel!

Bootstrap
Takeaways

Keep a Journal

1. Listen to your inner voice—in fact, write down what it's saying. Keep a journal to capture your thoughts, feelings, and ideas.

2. The secret is to buy a special journal or notebook that you want to write in. Spend some time picking out the right book; it will make a difference.

3. If the free-form diary approach isn't your style, try writing bulleted notes to yourself—that counts if it's a regular habit!

18

I Have a Theory

Study Great Leadership Thinking

WHETHER YOU'VE BEEN A LEADER for two years or twenty, you've probably learned a lot of what you know through experience. The lessons of experience are the best kind; you learn by doing, by making a few mistakes and adjusting your behavior accordingly. The more times you encounter a certain leadership situation, the better chance you have of responding to it with patience, skill, and confidence.

Although there's no substitute for on-the-job learning, there is something that can enhance your leadership capability, something that will add color and meaning to your experiences: a working knowledge of the classic models, frameworks, and theories of leadership. If you want to excel at setting strategy, managing people, and getting things done, you need to know something about the origins of human behavior and the best leadership practices. In fact, there are certain models and theories that *every* leader should know. Here are four theories to get you started (you can research others on the Internet; see Chapter 24). These four models substantially explain employee behavior, and a thorough understanding of them will make you a better leader. Indeed, if you manage people, you need to be familiar with these classics (and how to apply them) as you work to understand and relate to your employees.

Why Are They Doing That?

Like most leaders, you've probably been mystified on occasion by your people. Sometimes your employees act irrationally or become overly emotional, and it's hard to figure out exactly what's motivating them. Do you ever find yourself thinking: "Why are my employees so crazy?" or "What's wrong with these people?" You've been there, right? In reality, they're just acting according to the script; but do you know why? Abraham Maslow, Frederick Herzberg, David McClelland, and Fritz Heider do. And you can too if you familiarize yourself with their models of human behavior.

Let's start with Maslow's Hierarchy of Needs.[8] First conceived in 1943, Maslow's model still drives motivational theory today. Maslow created a theory of human needs that builds like a pyramid from the ground up; the model says that we all seek to satisfy *physiological* needs first (shelter, food, water) and then move through three more stages of need (*safety, belonging,* and *self-esteem*) before achieving the ultimate stage, *self-actualization.* Maslow's theory can help you understand what's motivating your people in different situations (e.g., a layoff or downsizing) and can explain why employees are slow to embrace change. When you know what stage of need your people are focused on, you can make adjustments in your communications or management style to accommodate them.

In 1958, Heider published his Attribution Theory, a model of how people ascribe meaning to the world around them.[9] Heider believed that people either assigned causality to *external attributions* (outside agents, factors, or forces) or *internal attributions* (things that fall within their control). This is the internal/external locus of control model, and it is a very useful way of understanding how people view events. Attribution Theory explains many of the defensive and negative attitudes that you encounter as a leader.

If you have an employee who struggles and sees everything as someone else's fault, this model can help you to get that person to accept that some of the issues are a result of his or her own behaviors or attitude.

In 1959, Herzberg published his Two Factor Theory, which builds on Maslow's work.[10] The Two Factor Theory states that satisfaction and psychological growth are the result of two categories of motivation, which Herzberg called *hygiene factors* and *motivator factors*. Herzberg stated that people first seek to satisfy hygiene factors, such as safety, salary, status, working conditions, and so forth, before they can or will be driven by motivators such as achievement, advancement, and increased responsibility. Again, as a leader, you need to be aware of how employees rank order their satisfiers; trying to motivate people with growth opportunities is tough if they're worried about their next paycheck.

Finally, in 1961, McClelland expanded on the motivation research by creating a framework he called the Theory of Needs, which describes people as being driven by three primary needs: 1) the *Need for Achievement*, 2) the *Need for Affiliation*, and 3) the *Need for Power*. [11] McClelland theorized that people can be categorized in terms of one of these three broad areas. The Thematic Apperception Test (TAT) provides a measure of this model and is still a popular leadership coaching tool. Think of someone you know up the chain of command in your company, and it's easy to form an immediate perception of their dominant need. In fact, it might be a good idea to know your dominant need, because it's probably driving a lot of your decisions. It also helps to know where your direct reports are coming from as you try to coach and develop them for future roles.

Studying the classic models, frameworks, and theories of leadership isn't just for "leadership nerds"; anyone serious about becoming a true student of leadership should know the basics of human behavior. You should not only know these theories (in addition to others you can research on your own) but you should also teach them to your team. In your regular staff meetings, take one theory at a time and discuss it as a group. One approach is to make it a development assignment for your team members, and have them do the research and lead the discussion. However you end up using the knowledge, make an effort to learn the theories and models that shape your world as a people manager. You'll definitely be smarter about the foundations of leadership, which in turn will help you break out of the pack and get noticed within the organization. You wouldn't mind being known as a leadership guru, would you?

Bootstrap
Takeaways

Study Great Leadership Thinking

1. Get curious about the topic of leadership. Learn the foundational theories that explain human behavior.
2. Familiarize yourself with the best practices of leadership by studying the models or frameworks that describe classic processes or tools.
3. Become a student *and* a teacher: Pass these models and theories on to your team and challenge them to do the research and the debriefs.

19

Once Upon a Time

Become a Great Storyteller

WHEN'S THE LAST TIME you heard a really great speech from one of your organization's senior leaders? How'd he or she do? Were you engaged? Did you understand the intended message, and could you translate that for your team? Was any part of it truly memorable? How did it land with the rest of the audience—could you tell? The fact is leaders often find themselves speaking or presenting in front of an audience of employees, trying to deliver a particular message. You've probably been in front of your own team several times this year. How'd you do? Are you happy with your speaking or presenting style? Did you have a specific purpose in mind, and did you achieve it? Though it helps to have persuasive facts, a compelling message, and a clear sense of the appropriate steps to take, there's one other element you should add to your toolkit if you want to be an effective public speaker: the art of telling stories.

By now it's common knowledge that storytelling is a great way for leaders to convey a message, share their experiences, and inspire an audience. Storytelling, of course, has a long and rich history. Humans have been telling stories for as long as they've been communicating; stories were the primary means of teaching and sharing wisdom before writing was invented. Whether they captured real experiences or were merely fables or parables, stories were passed down from generation to generation as a way of preserving precious memories and sharing knowledge. Isn't it remarkable that the oldest means of communicating a message is still one of the best?

Stories serve to flesh out or illustrate your message, making it easier to remember. Stories add color and texture to your key points, giving people a way to relate to what you're saying or asking them to do. Listen to just about any speech, and when your attention starts to drift, notice if you snap right back when the speaker starts to tell a story. That's the power of stories; we're programmed from a young age to perk up and listen to a story, waiting to see how it will end. In fact, stories will be what your audience or team remembers about the speech or presentation, long after the PowerPoint slides have faded or your statistics have grown outdated. Stories simply stick with people, and they provide an easy way for leaders to cascade a message to their teams. Telling a story isn't hard, of course; you do it several times each day without even thinking about it. But there is an art to weaving stories into your message; it takes a little imagination and planning. Following are four techniques to use when adding stories to your next speech or presentation.

Connect Stories to Your Key Messages

First, be sure to connect the story to your key messages. There's no magic formula to the number of stories you can tell in any one speech, but you're probably striving to make two or three main points, at best. Make sure each of your main points has a story to help drive the message home. Let me tell you a story to illustrate how this works (see how easy this is?). A few years ago, our HR team was launching a new internal marketing slogan. We were looking to boost our own customer focus skills by using the phrase "moments that matter" to describe our desired interaction with employees (we wanted every encounter with the HR team to be a meaningful touch point for our associates). I was one of several senior HR leaders who spoke that day in support of this new initiative, and I shared the story of a book I was reading called *Once Upon a Town* by Bob Greene.[12] The book is about the citizens of North Platte, Nebraska, who opened a 24-hour canteen at their train station to bring a little joy to the thousands of U.S. soldiers who were moving through on troop trains during WW II. What was remarkable about the story was that the trains only stopped in North Platte for about fifteen minutes. In those brief moments, however, in the middle of nowhere, the soldiers experienced an outpouring of love and generosity that would stay with them for years. The spirit of "making every associate interaction count" really came alive with the help of this example. I was able to use a story to connect to the key message, which helped people understand what we were trying to do. Afterward, I received a lot of positive feedback from the audience about my story; most people told me it helped them emotionally connect with the initiative we were trying to drive. What's the moral of *this* particular story? Matching your stories to your key messages brings your main points to life.

Second, build a well-crafted story. As with any story, be sure it has a beginning, a middle, and an end; make it easy to follow. Introduce the story by saying: "Let me tell you a story to demonstrate this" or "Here's a story that illustrates what I'm talking about." Then clearly state how the story actually does connect to your message (stories don't work if they leave your audience scratching their heads for relevance).

Third, in today's world, it's important to ensure that the story is culturally and politically correct. You don't need the awkward moment that comes with putting your foot in your mouth by sharing a story that will offend any portion of the audience. This goes double for stories that you think are cute or funny; keep it clean, or don't tell it at all.

Finally, keep your story short; the best stories take only a minute or two to deliver. Get into your story, make your points, and move on. If you ramble along for ten minutes with a poorly constructed story, you'll lose the audience—so keep it brief, but tell it with passion.

What type of stories work best? Examples from your own experience always get high marks, especially if they're representing you in a humble or "I learned from my mistakes" perspective. Lessons from great leaders throughout history work well, too, to illustrate what other leaders struggled with or achieved. Clearly, lessons learned within your own organization are a big hit because they're so relevant.

Even ancient fables or parables work and can be a lot of fun to share. Just make sure they're connected to your message (you might seek feedback from a few peers to see if they see the same link you do).

One of the best ways to pull yourself up by your own bootstraps is to make yourself into a better public speaker. Developing your storytelling capability will help you get there. The next time you have a speech or a presentation to give, find room for a few stories, and watch your audience respond when you say those six magical words: "Let me tell you a story. . . ."

Bootstrap
Takeaways

Become a Great Storyteller

1. Add stories to your next speech or presentation, and start using the power of storytelling to connect with your audience.
2. Use stories that obviously connect to your key messages. Don't make your audience search for relevance—make the metaphor clear.
3. Become known as a great storyteller and people will actually look forward to seeing you up on stage. Imagine that!

20

This Is Me

Share Your Leadership Foundations

THERE ARE TWO KINDS of people in the world: those who liked art class as children and those who were absolutely terrified of art class. Do you remember art class? Oh man, talk about separating the creative types from the mere mortals. For many of us, this is where our artistic phobia was born; our drawings looked like Salvador Dali paintings, we couldn't get the glue to work, and any kind of subjective assignment totally freaked us out. If you're the visually creative type, bless you—keep doing your thing. The world needs more people who can take a box of crayons, a few pipe cleaners, and some sparkly buttons and turn them into something beautiful. As for the rest of us, we crave direction and the structure of letters and words. Pictures aren't our thing; we communicate with language, not visuals.

You know you're in one of these two camps—don't even try to hide it. Put it this way: Do you like to play games that require you to draw? Thought so; nothing much has changed since the second grade, right? And this has carried over into your work life, yes? Well, whether you're artistic or can't draw a stick figure, this next challenge has something for you. You can use either talent to build your leadership skills. And no matter how you do this, it's going to come out perfect, because it's going to be all about you.

Here's the idea: You're going to represent yourself in words and drawings on a single sheet of blank paper. Ready, begin! Just kidding—I'll give you a little more direction than that (just wanted to mess with all you structured types). First of all, any size paper will work; you can start with regular copy paper, but if you're really ambitious, you can do this on a poster board and tap into your artistic side. OK, got your paper and a pencil or pen? That's all you need—now, just fill up the page with information that defines and describes who you are as a person (see Figure 5). Start writing and drawing whatever comes to mind; capture things that would help someone understand you or tell the story of your personal journey. Where did you come from? What lessons did you learn early on that shaped your values? What's important to you—why are you working? What inspires you? What are your passions, and how do they impact how you see the world? Anything that says: "This is me—this is what I'm all about" is perfect for this exercise.

What's Your Unique Story?

I first saw this technique used by Karl Werwath, who was a senior executive at a company where I was serving as the head of learning and leadership development. We had invited Karl to be a speaker at our high-potential leadership program because we knew he was a role model for servant leadership and living the company's values. Everyone knew Karl was a great leader, so we were eager to hear what he had to say about managing complex organizations and leading change. Now, when preparing for these sessions, we always asked to see the executives' slides, so we could sync up messages and keep them on track. When we met with Karl, he said he wanted to tell a few stories, and oh yeah, he had one slide he wanted to share, but he would bring that with him to hand out. When we asked if we could see it, he looked at us with a twinkle in his eye, and said: "Just trust me; I've used it for years, and people seem to like it. I'll bring it to the session."

So we trusted him, and I'm sure glad we did. Karl turned in one of the top-rated sessions we'd ever had, and to my knowledge, is still teaching the same session today. You know why it's so popular? Because he just tells stories and talks from his heart about leadership and what it means to him. He talks about his parents and the lessons they taught him that he still uses as a leader. He talks of his family and his hobbies and how they provide much-needed balance to his hectic work life. He encourages participants to ground themselves in their own values, and he caps off the session by handing out his version of this document. Then he takes the group through it with humility and passion. It's a magical session, and participants love it. I remember my astonishment at the document's simplicity and elegance, and I asked him after the session what he called it. Karl just shrugged his shoulders and said: "I don't really have a name for it. When I give it to new people who join my team I just say: 'This is me. I want you to know where I'm coming from, because this is how you'll experience my leadership.'" That weekend, I took out a piece of paper and wrote my own "this is me" document (Figure 5). I suppose one could update this document from time to time as they gain new perspectives, but I haven't found the need to do so; today everything on this page is just the way I wrote it years ago. Like Karl's document, this was my first and only version—and that's part of the beauty of the exercise.

Why would you want to do this? I think the question is, why wouldn't you? Talk about adding something cool to your leadership toolkit—it makes you think about what's truly important, and the document is a great way to share your leadership foundation with others. Have fun and get creative with this; you might choose different buckets or headings or use more drawings to share your story. In the end, you're creating a one-page time capsule of who you are, which explains why and how you show up as a leader. Once you've got it the way you want it, share it with your team; encourage them to make their own pages, and go outside on a beautiful day and share them with each other.

No matter your level of creativity, you can't miss with this exercise. And just imagine how proud you would make your second-grade art teacher!

Bootstrap
Takeaways

Share Your Leadership Foundations

1. Who are you? Think about everything that is important to you, and write or draw it on one page.
2. Share the document with your team, peers, boss, and others. Let them in on what drives and inspires you.
3. Use your "This Is Me" document as a teaching tool. It's a great way to talk about work-life balance and your priorities.

Part Three

Get Curious about the World Around You

NOW THAT YOU'VE ACQUIRED some new leadership skills, it's time to branch out and expand your horizons. Developing yourself as a leader also means stretching your point of view and seeing beyond the borders of your office (and company). The world is shrinking, but you need to broaden your perspective. As you move up the ladder in your organization, you're going to be expected to see the world through a much wider lens. And if you think your company is going to do this for you, think again. You need to do this for yourself.

Let's start with your general business acumen. How current are you with new developments in your field? Are you proactive, or do you make do with the latest ideas that happen to fall into your lap? Do you have a firm grasp of your organization's strategy? Do you know what people do in other parts of the company? How about your competitors: Do you know what they're up to? Just imagine if you were asked to give a ten-minute presentation this afternoon on your company's top five competitors and their comparative strengths and weaknesses. Would you be prepared or would you be afraid of embarrassing yourself? C'mon, you're a leader in the firm—surely you might be expected to know this kind of stuff. What about looking beyond your industry: What's happening in organizations that look nothing like yours? What can you learn from them? Get creative, and tap into your supplier or vendor contacts, or reach out to your vast network to find and share these best practices. What's that? You don't have a vast professional network? Then it's time to build one, don't you think? Are you working the social networks on the Internet or attending conferences and seminars to expand your worldview?

How about learning about cultures other than your own? If you don't have people of different nationalities working for you now, you probably will soon. While you're at it, take a deep interest in your current team; get to know them on a deeper level. That is, unless you enjoy the view from your desk. Then you can probably skip these chapters. I'm sure the company has plenty of leaders who'd be happy to pass you by. After all, it's only your career!

21

Take a Trip Around the World

Learn about Other Cultures

IF YOU MANAGE PEOPLE, there's a good chance you have someone on your team who doesn't look like you. Not exactly like you, of course—that would be weird. I'm referring to different cultures here. You know, people with different life experiences, who don't share your background and didn't walk the same path you traveled.

The first time you manage someone from an unfamiliar culture, it can be a bit intimidating, both for you and for the employee. You may have different value systems, religious beliefs, family traditions, food preferences—you name it. There may be a language barrier or a work ethic issue that causes you to communicate or set performance goals differently. Or maybe you don't share the same macropolitical views, which can make agreeing on business strategy a real challenge. Whatever the cultural differences, sometimes meshing with people from different backgrounds can be frustrating, for both parties.

Because you're the manager, you have an obligation to overcome the cultural divide that can inhibit a normal working relationship. Yes, employees share responsibility for making things work; they should be accountable for adhering to company policies and generally adapting to the work environment. But as the leader, you have a higher calling; it's your job to leverage the unique contributions of *every* employee and create a high-performing team that maximizes results. You also should be focused on helping every employee realize his or her potential. That's hard to do if you don't know where your employees are coming from or what they value.

Learn a New Culture

By now, you can probably guess where this is going. In order to relate to and effectively manage people of different backgrounds, you need to learn about their way of life. If you want to cultivate a positive, tolerant workplace, you have to role-model an understanding and acceptance of other cultures. If you want to get the most out of training and development, you have to know what motivates people (for more on getting to know your people, see Chapter 25).

In short, you need to do your homework, and get curious about the world around you. This is one of the best (and most rewarding) ways you can develop yourself as a leader. If you've been avoiding this because a) you think others should adapt to you, or b) you're just too lazy to do the research, then think again; you're missing a great opportunity. Take advantage of the diversity on your team; leverage the differences of thought, style, and ideas that team members from other cultures have to offer. The results are worth the effort, and it starts with taking the time to get to know their world.

Learn their cultural norms. Find a way to learn about the key cultural aspects of their society. Knowledge of what is acceptable or taboo in a particular culture can go a long way toward strengthening relationships. People from different cultures have different ways of dealing with other people, celebrating success and accepting feedback. Learn these nuances and use them to manage your employees more effectively, including how others interact with them. For example, in some cultures, it's considered polite to let a team member offer an extended monologue in a staff meeting, without interruption. If one of your employees is struggling with the fast-paced, everyone-talk-at-once nature of your meetings, cultural norms might explain why they are reluctant to jump in and contribute. Don't assume this person isn't smart enough or quick enough and instead look at the underlying norms; there may be a deep-seated cultural reason why this employee is struggling to adapt.

An easy way to learn about other cultures is to read a book or search the Internet for specific content (try to search for work-related norms and behaviors, although an understanding of the broader society is important, too). One very important cultural element is religion, which helps explain many specific behaviors and beliefs. *The World's Religions* by Huston Smith is a wonderful source you can use to familiarize yourself with any of the seven major religions around the world.[13] Trust me, this book is worth reading.

Here's another way to learn: Simply sit down with your employees and express an interest in learning more about their cultures. Ask permission to inquire about their backgrounds; explain your desire to understand their cultures better, so you can make better connections and help them succeed. They'll probably be glad you asked, and will likely enjoy talking about the cultural differences that make working in your world a unique challenge. Be prepared to listen and ask probing questions to really understand the key points of differentiation. Do this over several sessions, so you can understand their cultures on a deeper level.

Understand the relationship between their cultures and your management style. Whether you are learning to manage a single employee or an entire team in a foreign market, you need to adapt your style to fit their culture in certain ways. Although it's true that you can't adapt everything to individual needs, leaders do need to be flexible and adapt their styles to accommodate cultural norms. For example, taking the entire team to task over a specific issue might be acceptable in some cultures but insulting in others. Scheduling work-related social events after hours might be fine for some employees but may make others uncomfortable. Putting people into teams, when they thrive on individual work (and vice versa) might not be the best way to make the most of their individual talents.

Take stock of your own management style, and look for opportunities to be more sensitive to cultural differences. You might start by learning a few words in your employee's native language (even using simple words and phrases such as "please," "thank you," and "good morning" goes a long way toward demonstrating your willingness to learn about their culture). Or, you might learn about the various holidays or special events that are probably being underappreciated around your office. For example, if you were to acknowledge Ramadan or Yom Kippur, think how favorably it would be received by employees who observe those holidays. Your employees will notice and appreciate your interest.

Leverage your cultural knowledge for the company as a whole. Learning about other cultures will serve you well as a people manager, no doubt. But it will also stamp you as a big-picture leader who "gets" globalization and the ever-changing marketplace. How can you leverage what you learn about other cultures for the good of the organization? How can your knowledge help build better products, customize services, or develop deeper talent pipelines? Can you start a grassroots campaign that opens up a new market or customer base? Look around you and combine your knowledge of different cultures with business or process opportunities you see across the company.

Put another way, if you can demonstrate that you have a working knowledge of various cultures, what doors might that open for you inside the company? Might you be seen as a more inclusive leader, one who has taken the time to add a new dimension to your game? You bet you will. And in today's world, this is important. If you take the time to learn about other cultures and leverage this knowledge to do great things around the company, someone will notice.

The most important thing in managing people of different cultures is to have an open mind. Respect is the lubricant of a smooth-running team; if you demonstrate a respect for the cultures of the people who work for you, you'll end up managing them more effectively, building a stronger team, and developing yourself in the process. That helps others perform better and helps raise your profile as a leader. And those are two pretty compelling reasons to dust off your research skills and do your homework.

Bootstrap
Takeaways

Learn about Other Cultures

1. If you manage employees with different backgrounds, make an effort to learn their cultures; conduct in-depth research to get a good working knowledge of their norms and traditions.
2. Set an example for others. Be a role model for diversity and cultural sensitivity.
3. Expand your knowledge to the company as a whole. Consider ways you can leverage this information to help the organization grow and succeed.

22

So *This* Is What We Do

Learn the Business

DO YOU WANT TO KNOW a little secret about large organizations? There are "front-line" employees that actually interact with customers, and then there are "back office" or headquarters employees who, well, don't engage with customers at all. The secret is, a lot of large-company employees (including many leaders) don't have a firm grasp on how the company really works. The organization is so large, and employees and managers are so busy with their own function or department, that they don't take the time (or aren't interested enough) to gain a deep understanding of how the company makes money. Oh, they know what business the company is in, and they probably know the main products or services. But ask them about specific details of customer service, finance, or manufacturing, and they might just shrug their shoulders. They haven't taken the time to learn the business.

Now, if you work in a smaller company, you may find this somewhat shocking. You might be thinking: "How could you not know how the company makes its product or interacts with customers? How could you not know critical financial details such as profit margin, price per unit, or cost of sales?" Of course, leaders in large-company operating units probably *do* have a clear sense of how the company works, and the finance leaders probably have a good handle on how the money is made. But the fact is, you can get by for several years elsewhere in a large company and never be asked to really learn the business. It's true—I've seen it (and even lived it). If you've ever worked in a large corporation, you probably know what I'm talking about.

No matter what size company you work in, if you don't know the basics of how your company manages to stay in business, you've got some work to do. This is leadership self-development of the most desperate kind; you don't want people to discover just how little you know, do you? Wouldn't it be a bit embarrassing to be a leader in the company and not have a good grasp of how the company works? If this resonates with you, if you realize you don't know as much as you should about your company, you need to turn this around quickly. Here's how to do it.

Get on the Front Lines

Your quest for knowledge can start in several places, of course. First, are you actually reading the annual report, or is it just sitting there on your credenza to make you look good? Uh, yeah, this just in: You're supposed to read it. It's not just for auditors and recruits; thumb through it and take away some nuggets about how the company works (not to mention how well it's doing). Second, read your company's external (and internal) Web sites. Click all around those sites for new facts or interesting tidbits (like that new expansion or acquisition that was just announced). Familiarize yourself with the bios of the senior team and board members. The leaders above you know these people, and there's no reason you shouldn't know them, too. Also, check out who's moving around inside the company; it's a good idea to know the current organizational chart. Third, find a peer in one of the lines of business and ask him or her to tutor you on the product or customer life cycle. Ask a friend or colleague in the finance department to do the same where the balance sheet is concerned (see Chapter 36). This is an easy way to pick up some of the finer points about the business, and you'll have the added bonus of developing relationships along the way. Another way to learn about the company is to contact administrators of the corporate university or learning center and ask about their "business fundamentals" courses. Chances are they offer some e-learning courses about how the company operates; you can take them in your spare time and start impressing people with your business acumen. Better yet, they might offer a classroom experience that's perfect for your whole team.

These are good techniques for getting up to speed about the company, and you should use them all on a regular basis (even if it's just to stay current). But nothing beats a visit to the front lines for a firsthand look at what your company does and how its business is conducted. That's right—if you really want to learn how the company operates and makes money, get out of your office and immerse yourself in what life is like where the company meets its customers.

Find out if your company has an employee immersion program, where you can arrange to work alongside front-line coworkers. If so, set up a day or two for you and your team, and turn it into a shared experience and learning opportunity. In my career, I've been fortunate to have two such experiences. At PepsiCo, where I worked in the Pizza Hut division, we were encouraged to spend several days each year working in the restaurants. Now you can imagine how skilled and useful I was (the answers are "not much" and "not very"), but the employees graciously took me under their wings and showed me the ropes. I do feel badly for the customers who got a pizza that I prepared, but I learned more about our business from that experience than I did in a year of sitting in meetings. It was a terrific opportunity to see how our training and HR policies were working, and I brought back several good ideas and lessons learned. Likewise, when I was at Capital One, our team participated in a program whereby corporate executives could sit with customer service representatives to answer real customer calls. Talk about scary! We were petrified, but we got through it (again, with the help of some outstanding employees) and we learned a great deal about the issues facing both our customers and those terrific front-line representatives. We took away a healthy respect for what it means to know our business—and let me tell you, the customer service people in your company know your business!

If your company doesn't have a formal program, arrange somehow to "get out there" on a route ride, a sales call, or a night in the stores. Listen in to calls with customers (the good and the bad) and visit the shop floor to see how the product is made. Talk to employees; find out the little details that explain profit margin or net income. Strive to learn what makes the company tick—how it really works. Then, use that knowledge to make adjustments in your plans, budgets and proposals. I guarantee you'll see your own job differently once you see others' up close. Experience the front lines of your business this month. You'll feel better about yourself, you'll feel more connected to the company, and you won't have to worry about your ability to answer a business question at your next staff meeting. You'll have facts to share and stories to tell—and that's something every leader should be able to do.

Bootstrap
Takeaways

Learn the Business

1. Do you know everything you should about your company? If not, change that with a targeted effort to learn the business.

2. Visit the front lines of the organization; find out how the product is made, how the service is delivered.

3. Bring your experiences back to your job. What opportunities did you see? Where can you and your team add more value and make a bigger impact?

23

Keep Tabs on Your Friends

Document Your Network

BY NOW YOU'VE FIGURED out that you can't improve your leadership skills completely on your own. The very essence of being a leader means interacting with others; that's why you got into this business, to work with people (yes, it's right there in the job description). The fact is, you need other people—and not just to have someone to lead. You need others to provide feedback, ideas, and encouragement. You need people to exchange information with, to seek answers from, and to connect you with *other* people. Perhaps most important, you need people who will say nice things about you if you ever need a recommendation (who hasn't experienced that lately?). In short, if you want to pull yourself up by your own bootstraps and develop your leadership skills, it helps to have a wealth of other people to draw on for support (for more on assessing your network, see Chapter 2).

By this point, you know all about the importance of networks; you've been reminded of this since you entered the workforce. But especially now, and especially as a leader, you need to network, network, network (by the way, you know a concept has reached critical importance when it becomes a verb as well as a noun). If you're already a great networker, if you have lots of contacts and work hard to keep them current, good for you. If not, it's generally because you don't like networking, you're too busy to do it, or you don't feel you need to meet new people. It's one of those reasons, isn't it? Go ahead, I'll wait—pick out your reason (be honest now). OK, have you identified the issue? Great, now let's explore a technique that may change your approach to networking.

Start with a List

You may be getting the feeling that every exercise begins with a list, and in this case, you'd be right. Make a list of everyone you know in the world of business—absolutely everyone. Include every person you've ever met or worked with; go back to your earliest jobs and companies and write down the names of people you'd like to reconnect with, stay in touch with, or just keep tabs on (see Chapter 8). Add to the list anyone that you *want* to meet or work with, including people in your current company, but also vendors, recruiters, business partners, clients, contacts, authors, etc. Don't stop until you can't think of another person that you know, need to know, or would like to know. (Obviously, you might want to stretch this exercise out over several weeks—this could take awhile!) Put all of the names together in a document that you can access easily, and start taking control of your network.

I use a simple spreadsheet to manage my network, and I recommend it as a convenient way to keep track of people and plan your networking activities. First, arrange your network into meaningful groups, such as previous companies, vendors, trade associations, and so forth; it helps to "bucket" people into categories of when and how you met them. Following their names, create a column labeled "Then" to indicate how you knew (or know) them by documenting their role and company. Then, because people often change jobs, create a "Now" column to indicate what role and company they're in now. Use the next two columns to record their current contact information (label these columns "Email" and "Phone"). Then (and this is the key column) create a "Last Contact" column to make a note of the last time you heard from them. Only put a date in this column if you truly made contact with them—you want a record of your network hits and not merely the attempts. Next, organize yourself by planning your next contact: When are you going to reach out to them again? Label this column "Next Contact." Finally, create a "Notes" column to capture what you talked about or any other pertinent information you want to document.

Use the List Every Day

Open and use your network spreadsheet every day. Literally, there shouldn't be a day that goes by that you do not update the list. Every time you touch base with a contact, update the "Last Contact" column. And then immediately document when you plan to connect with them again by filling in the "Next Contact" column (I like to touch base with everyone in my network at least twice a year, so I plan my next contact accordingly). Keep the contact information up-to-date at all times; when someone moves or gets a new phone number or email address, change it on your list (this takes work; don't get lazy with this or you'll lose track of people—and your network is useless if it is out of date). Another trick you might find useful is to document how you know certain people. I use the "Now" column to make notes to myself about where I met someone or who introduced us. In the "Notes" column, write down anything that you think will help you remember conversations, obligations, key connection points, etc. I sometimes capture how I feel about the relationship or make a note of what I want to accomplish next time (I may want to reach out more often or ask for a favor).

There's something about the *process* of organizing your network that makes it come alive for you. Use this technique to go back in time and find old friends and colleagues that you used to work with (sign on to social networking Web sites such as Facebook and LinkedIn and start tracking them down). Use it to keep track of business contacts outside of your company—the ones you'd forget to call or write otherwise (these contacts are critical, especially if you need a wide network to help you find your next job). Use it to expand the list of people you know inside the company; in fact, you can "pre-populate" the list and then use it as inspiration to start meeting those people so you can update their information in the spreadsheet!

How many people should you have in your network? The simple answer is: as many as you can. When you reach out to reconnect with people, don't worry that you won't have anything to say or that you're pestering them with calls or emails. They'll let you know whether (and how often) they want to maintain contact through their actions. Use your own judgment about how many times to reach out before crossing them off your list (I never cross anyone off the list entirely, but I do "gray out" the names of people who just won't take the time to connect). Who should be in your network? Anyone that you a) want to stay in touch with, b) need to have a relationship with to get work done, or c) feel you can help (or can help you) now or sometime in the future.

Like a lot of leadership skills, networking is an art—and art requires you to put your own personal stamp on it. You're smart, so you know these relationships won't maintain themselves. You have to work at meeting and staying in touch with people. Turn your network into a working document, and manage it daily. Get organized and planful about your relationship building, and challenge yourself to build (and use) a stronger network. After all, you never know when you're going to need it.

Bootstrap
Takeaways

Document Your Network

1. Create and maintain a healthy network of business colleagues and contacts. Start by writing down the name of everyone you know or should know.

2. Put your network into a "working document" that you use on a daily basis. Make updating your network a regular routine.

3. Use your network proactively and strategically. Get planful and organized about who you're contacting and why.

24

That Thing Called the Internet

Leverage Technology

OK, WE CAN'T AVOID this conversation any longer. Let's cut to the chase: I'm going to take a wild stab here and guess that you're under-leveraging the greatest learning tool of our lifetime. Maybe you've heard of it. It's a little thing I like to call the Internet. You probably even know how to use it—you Google or Bing what you what to know and, like magic, the answer appears. The great thing about the Internet is that it's like a twenty-four-hour a day ATM for information; you can find anything, anytime, just about any-where. But are you leveraging it fully as a leadership development tool? Are you using the Web to proactively grow as a leader? Are you *strategically* using the Internet to help you improve your lead-ership skills?

Let's start by assuming that you stay up-to-date on the daily news, through any number of sources: newspapers, radio, TV, mobile devices, etc. (if you're not, then you should be). The Inter-net is famous for this, of course—it's where more and more people go to keep up with breaking news. But are you using the Internet to develop deeper knowledge or build skills? Are you using the Web to access new points of view, inform or change your opin-ions, and to gather research and get ideas for leading more effectively? Making the Internet work for you is an art, one you can easily master if you have the curiosity and discipline to do a little homework. Here are three ways to use the Internet to become a better leader.

Do You Have the Discipline?

First, use the Internet to add depth to your knowledge base. Find four online sources for commentary and information, bookmark them, and then (and here's the hard part) actually read them on a regular basis. Yeah, that last point got your attention, didn't it? Actually checking the sources on a consistent schedule takes incredible discipline, it's true. But you can do it if you put your mind to it. Here's my approach. For *weekly* check-ins, I pick the same time each week to log on and skim my favorite sites (for me, it's Sunday night while preparing for the week ahead). For *monthly* content, I use my birthday date, which serves as a mental reminder for me (I check my bookmarks on the twenty-first of each month). Checking the monthly publications on the same date each month also assures me of finding new material to read.

I recommend choosing one source for weekly world news, one for weekly business news, one for a monthly check-in on your industry or functional area, and one for a monthly review of leadership or coaching ideas. Find sites that will give you an unbiased perspective or that present different points of view. Yes, you'll need some time and discipline to accomplish this, but then nothing worthwhile comes without a little dedication. First, put in the time to find the right Web sites; look for compelling sources that you'll actually read (or skim) on a regular basis. It's important to not have too many sites bookmarked—that's a sure way to not read any of them (they become mere "references" in your mind). Stick to just four bookmarks, and read them on a consistent basis (you can always switch out when you find a better source). Label the folder "My Reading List" to boost its status on your favorites list. Get into a regular habit of skimming the four sources for "news you can use"; make it part of your development plan or ask a peer to hold you accountable for summarizing what you're learning online. Keeping current on the latest thinking and ideas isn't easy. This content won't magically find its way to your doorstep—you have to go looking for it, and once you find it, actually absorb it. Fortunately, the Internet is the world's largest library, and you have a lifetime membership. But you have to use it!

Your Source for Development Ideas

The second way to use the Internet is to research specific ideas or tips for your own development. Say you've gotten feedback that you need to listen or delegate more effectively. OK, but how do you *do* that? If you don't have a mentor or corporate university to assist you, go online and start researching recommendations for working on this skill. There is a lot of great content online for specific development opportunities. Look for sites that specialize in leadership content, and triangulate the advice from several different sources on a specific topic. Once you start reading the same suggestions over and over you can be pretty sure the advice is sound and grounded in multiple experiences. Look for credible sources such as respected executive coaches or consultants who post free development content online. Throughout this process, do not simply skim the material to stay current; take extensive notes and build a plan to put the ideas into practice. Bookmark these sources under specific folder names (e.g., Strategy, Listening, Coaching, etc.) so you can refer back to them from time to time. In essence, you're building your own resource center on specific leadership skills development, one that you can share with others who have the same opportunities.

Leverage Social Networks

Finally, plug into online, public forum networks devoted to leadership or your area of functional expertise. You're probably already on some of the business-related social networking sites such as LinkedIn or Plaxo, but are you leveraging them fully? Learning from others who are doing the same job or working on the same challenges can be a great way to broaden your horizons and push your thinking. Are you accessing other people directly for best practices or new ideas? Do you belong to any online networks to exchange information on processes and tools? Join a local, national, or worldwide forum, or if you're really ambitious, join two networks: one in your specific discipline (Finance, IT, Marketing, etc.) and one devoted to leadership. The Internet allows you to do "passive networking" at your pace and on your terms. Set aside some time to find the right networks to plug into, and then check in periodically to review the posted content and follow the discussion threads that have value for you. Who knows, you might establish some relationships that you can tap into more broadly going forward in your career.

It's out there, people—the greatest learning tool of all time. Be it information, research, or networking, you literally have the world at your fingertips, twenty-four hours a day. What are you doing to take advantage of it? Start surfing with a purpose: Get strategic about how you're leveraging the Internet. The world is waiting for you!

Bootstrap
Takeaways

Leverage Technology

1. Commit to a routine of using the Internet proactively to drive your own development.

2. Take charge of your own learning: Find content that moves you forward in terms of knowledge and insight.

3. Expand your horizons by establishing new relationships: Join an online leadership forum or network.

25

Who Are These People?

Get to Know Your Team Members

LEADERSHIP IS ABOUT OTHER PEOPLE. You can't truly be a leader if you don't enlist other people to help you get things done. The simple truth is that leaders need people as much as people need leadership; it's hard to accomplish anything of great magnitude alone. Great leaders understand this, and work hard to empower, develop, and take care of their people. And it all starts with getting to know them—beyond simply their status as employees.

How well do you know your people? When you have direct reports, or an extended team, you need to really understand what makes each one of them unique. Where do they come from? What gets them excited? Why do they work for you? People want to be connected to their manager and their companies in ways that go beyond the transaction of work. When you don't take a personal interest in your people, you can't fully capture their hearts and minds; you may be able to get their commitment to the task at hand, but you won't be able to build the kind of high-performing team that is fully dedicated to you and the mission. True leadership starts with taking a genuine interest in your people.

There's an easy way to get to know your people better: Simply ask them questions about themselves. This goes beyond asking about how the weekend went on Monday morning (although this is a fine question, make sure you're truly interested; otherwise it will come off as silly and disingenuous). If you're a new manager or you're taking over a new group of people, set up a series of personal interviews with your staff and their staff (see Chapter 44) to get to know them as people and not just as cogs in the wheel. You can do this no matter how many people you have in your group. Michael Abrashoff, retired Naval Commander and author of the wonderful book *It's Your Ship* interviewed all of the more than three hundred sailors aboard the *U.S.S. Benfold* when he first took command.[14] Abrashoff credits getting to know his crew as the key to turning the *Benfold* into the best ship in the Pacific Fleet. If Captain Abrashoff could interview more than three hundred people in his first hundred days, then certainly you can sit down with six direct reports when starting a new role!

OK, so it's easy if you're new to the group; but what do you do if you've been with your team for awhile? The technique is the same: personal interviews. Now if you've been the type of manager that has always taken an interest in your people, great; just explain that you want to get an even better understanding of their background and interests. However, if you've never shown much interest in your people before, then obviously there is going to be some skepticism. In this case, you have only one choice: You need to communicate that this is an area of development for you. Explain that you want to change this aspect of your leadership and that you'd like their help. If you really want to add this element to your game, you may need to eat a little humble pie, especially if you portray the image that you don't care about your people. Admitting that this has been a shortcoming in the past and asking the following five simple questions will go a long way toward turning that image around.

Gather Their Stories

1. **"Where (and how) did you grow up?"** Most people like to share their personal history—where they were born, how they grew up, what their parents did, and so forth. Take an interest in your employees' backgrounds; not only is it respectful, but you also might learn something useful in terms of managing them. For instance, people who grew up on farms generally have deep-seated views on values and work ethic; people who grew up in big, cosmopolitan cities generally are comfortable mixing it up with peers.

2. **"What are your hobbies?"** What do your people like to do when they're not working? Knowing a little about what gives them joy outside of work helps you relate to them more effectively. You might be able to draw a connection from a work project back to something they care deeply about in their personal lives. Again, take an interest in your people's lives outside of work.

3. **"Who's the most important person (people) in your life?"** Find out who they care most about, and learn their name(s). If your direct reports have children, learn all of their names. Knowing this single fact allows you to be sensitive to personal challenges outside of work that you might be able to help with; again, with all that your people do for you, knowing who is important to them is the least you can do.

4. **"What are you passionate about?"** What really motivates your people? Some people are really into sports, or politics, or volunteering in their communities. In your group, there might be a fascinating story about someone who runs her own nonprofit organization—what could you do with that information? You can learn a lot about people if you know what really inspires them.

5. **"What do you want to do with the rest of your life?"** The answers to this question offer countless insights, including whether you can help them make their dreams come true. What if you learned that someone always wanted to live abroad and you had the ability to make that happen with a transfer or job rotation?

Lastly, make this a purposeful exercise. Take notes as you conduct the interviews. I had to go into note-taking overdrive once when I had ten direct reports (which is far too many, by the way; it's time to reorganize when you have that many directs!). This was a rapidly changing environment, and it seemed like I was getting new team members every few months. I knew I wouldn't remember everything about each person (especially because they were turning over quickly), so I bought a special notebook just for these stories and later transferred the key information to index cards. I later reviewed those index cards before some of my one-on-one meetings. Whatever you may think of the "cheat sheet" approach, I had just one goal: I wanted to get the names and the situations right. I still didn't remember everything, and sometimes forgot to ask about crucial personal matters, but I made a determined effort to get certain details right. If you have a lot of direct reports, take my advice: Buy a stack of index cards.

The bottom line is to know your people. Ask them about themselves because a) you're interested, and b) you want to remember what's important to them. Make a sincere effort to learn these five things about each person that works for you; it will absolutely make you a better manager. Think of any boss you've ever had: Didn't you enjoy working for those who took a genuine interest in you as a person? Be that leader who truly cares about your people—you'll be amazed at the difference it makes in how others experience your leadership.

Bootstrap
Takeaways

Get to Know Your People

1. Take a genuine interest in your people—interview everyone on your team to unlock hidden skills or talents.
2. Be known as a leader who cares about and takes care of his or her people.
3. Be a role model for "managing by walking around." Make it clear that you understand that people make the difference.

26

Ask the Experts

Tap Vendors and Consultants for New Ideas

ONE OF THE TRAITS that distinguishes a great leader from an average one is intellectual curiosity. You have to keep up with the times to be a great leader—and that means being interested in the world around you. Great leaders seek an edge; they're constantly looking for ways to beat the competition or make the organization more efficient. That's why one of your challenges as a leader is to be constantly looking for new ideas. It should be a near obsession—how can we do things cheaper, better, faster? Within your scope of responsibility or your functional expertise, the company is counting on you for innovation; that's why you make the big bucks. Think about that for a second: They pay you to be curious. Not bad, huh? So how are you going to exercise this curiosity and thirst for new ideas? Well, you could sit around and ask your peers a bunch of questions, but that's no way to learn about what is happening outside the organization.

No, you can't just rely on your ability to be instantly brilliant; sometimes you have to do your homework. You can read or research what other companies are doing, of course—there is a lot of information out there about best practices. But do you have the time? And do you have a broad enough lens? Many leaders become obsessed with what their direct competitors, or other players in their broader industry, are doing. That's a good strategy, but the fact is, a lot of good ideas also come from looking at industries or markets that have nothing to do with yours. You need to look high and low for best practices and new ideas—at a variety of organizations—and that requires focus and resources. If only there was an easy way to see inside these other companies . . .

Turn Your Partners into Consultants

In reality, there is an easy way to see inside other companies. And the sources are already knocking on your door; all you have to do is let them in and put them to work. Most of you probably interact with vendors or business partners in one form or another. Well guess what? They work with a lot of other companies, too. Ask them if they'd be willing to come in and talk with you and your team about the best practices they're seeing in other companies. Most vendors will jump at the chance to strengthen their relationship with you and will be open to spending some time answering your questions. Obviously, there is some degree of confidentiality around sharing specific company information; you might learn the best practices but not get a good sense of where they are being applied. That's OK because you're interested mostly in the ideas. If you want to explore something specific, let them know in advance so they can tap into the right sources in their company. All it takes is a phone call with the simple question: "Could you please put together a presentation of the best practices at XYZ company?" Buy your vendors lunch, and have them brief you and the team on what they're seeing out there—that's more than a fair trade for some cutting edge information.

To maximize the potential impact, set up a panel discussion on a variety of topics and invite your whole team (or a group of peers) to join you. Make it a department-wide invitation, and you've got an employee development session (a seminar on best practices).

For example, if you're a leader in IT, there are probably dozens of vendors available to talk to you and the team about new hardware and software, the latest trends in data storage or records management, what the major developers are working on, and so on. Afterward, post the learnings and best practices on the internal Web portal and make it clear to everyone in your department when you learn something new about the outside world, you're expected to share it with the rest of the team by writing an article and posting it to the share drive. The point is, you have valued business partners that would be happy to sit down with you and brainstorm ways to make your business better. After all, they have a vested interest in seeing you innovate and evolve. Don't be shy about using this source to help you develop new ideas. I knew a leader who made this a quarterly event. She was a VP in Operations, and because they had several vendors that they worked with regularly, she simply rotated them through her normal all-hands meetings as development for her team. The vendors shared what they were seeing out in the marketplace and led a lively Q&A discussion. Her team looked forward to these sessions, as it gave them a chance to look outside the company and have a serious dialog about cutting-edge developments in their field.

Answer Those Consultant Calls

Another way to find out what's going on beyond your company is to return some of those consultant calls that are stacked up in your voice mail. As a manager, you probably receive many inquiries from consultants who want a few minutes of your time. How about inviting a few of them in to talk with you? What have you got to lose? You don't have to buy anything, you know. In the normal course of a one-hour sales meeting with a consultant, you can learn a lot about what's going on in the industry. When I led large learning and development teams in my corporate days, I always gave time to consultants. First of all, as a former consultant, I empathized with them; I know what it can mean to get a meeting and possibly get your foot in the door. But I didn't take all those meetings just to be nice; I did it to find out what they knew. I wanted to pick their brains. I wanted to find out who their clients were, what was selling in the marketplace. I wanted to hear their take on the best learning management systems, where they thought corporate universities were headed in the next five years, what they thought of virtual learning techniques, and so on. Invariably, we'd end up teaching each other, having a fruitful conversation, and advancing the relationship—a win for both parties.

If you need to work on your intellectual curiosity, think about sitting down with your current partners or meeting with that consultant who has been trying to get in to see you. Want to break out and take charge of your own development? Exchange a bit of your time for some valuable information and new ideas; it's a great way to accelerate your learning curve and build some lasting relationships in the process.

Bootstrap
Takeaways

Tap Vendors and Consultants for New Ideas

1. Feed your curiosity by meeting with your external business partners about "what they're seeing out there."
2. Take that meeting with the consultant who's been soliciting you. Let the consultant make the pitch, then ask a LOT of questions.
3. Make this a team thing—encourage everyone on your team to explore external best practices.

27

Scout the Enemy

Know Your Competitors

DO YOU EVER STOP to think about how far you've come? You've worked your whole life to get to this exact place, and you did it through hard work and perseverance. Take a moment to savor that, because no one will appreciate the journey more than you. It's probably not the last stop, either; you have a lot to accomplish yet in your career. There's that promotion up ahead that will help you break out of the pack, and you're busy getting a "double major" in your functional area and as a leader. Put it all together, and you're poised to make an even greater contribution to the organization. So, it's all good, right?

Well, maybe—unless, of course, there's something missing, something you're not paying attention to, either because you don't see it or because you're too busy. It's pretty important, too, and it will hold you back if you don't do something about it. Don't know what it is, do you? Want me to tell you? No, it's not your posture, your winning smile, or your style of clothes (although you should always sit up straight, put on a positive attitude, and dress sharp). Those are important, but not as important as this secret to moving up the leadership ladder: You need to become intimately familiar with the competition. If you don't take an interest in where your company stands in relation to your closest competitors, no one is going to take you seriously as an executive. There, I said it. Might be a little harsh, but it's the truth, so consider yourself warned. But it's never too late to start working on this aspect of your game so you can break out and get noticed by senior management.

Take an Interest in Your Competitors

Admit it: You don't know everything you could about the competition, do you? That's OK. Admission is the first step in making a behavior change. Heck, I'll admit it. I didn't always have a great working knowledge of the competition when I was in corporate America. For example, in the four years I spent at America Online, I never did develop a great sense of what Microsoft, NetZero, Earthlink, Yahoo!, and others were doing in the marketplace. Now, you could say that because I was in HR, it wasn't my job to know intricate details about these companies' business models or marketing strategies. But I wasn't spending enough time learning what they were doing in my own space; I didn't know much about their recruiting, training, and engagement processes, or how they approached high potentials, succession planning, and leadership development. Mind you, I knew some of the basics but not nearly enough. I'm not proud of this story, but I share it to illustrate how common it can be to put your head in the sand and just focus on your own company. Sure I could trot out a bunch of excuses: I was too busy, I didn't need to know these details to do my job, I knew enough to get by, and so forth. But frankly, that's exactly what those are—excuses. Would I have been a better thought leader, a better conduit of information for my team, a better executive, if I had developed a keen sense of the competition? You bet. And judging by conversations that I've had with hundreds of leaders over the years, I'm not alone here. So let's explore your approach to getting smart about the competition. Turns out you can know quite a bit about your competitors if you focus on just the following four pieces of information.

How Much Do You Know?

First, you need to know how the competition stacks up, that is, how they compare to your company relative to market positioning. How big a share of the market do they have? This information is generally available in analyst reports or on the Internet, and your own Finance Department probably keeps an updated lead table to track market share. Get your hands on this information, because this is one of the best ways to keep score when comparing companies and determining who's winning the battle for customers.

Second, try to learn and compare revenue and profit margin figures for the top companies in your industry. Who's making (and keeping) the most money? *Fortune* magazine's annual Fortune 500 list includes a good deal of information that you can easily absorb and share with your team.

Third, try to keep up to date on who's developing new products and services. Who's winning the innovation game? Set up an alert on your favorite search engine to get articles that tout your competition's latest inventions or processes (see Chapter 24).

Finally, try to get a sense of what your competitors are doing from an employment perspective. This will tell you who's winning the war for talent. *Fortune* magazine's Most Admired Companies and Best Companies to Work For lists will help you get a sense for this part of the equation.

When you can talk intelligently about these four factors—where your company stands relative to its competitors in terms of customers, financials, innovation, and employment practices—

you probably will be recognized as one of the most knowledgeable leaders in your organization when it comes to the "other guys" in your industry. So, are you interested? Do you have what it takes to commit to this "extra credit" work? No? Oh, I get it; you work *here,* and have your hands full just helping *this* company produce results. OK, that's fine; if you don't mind staying in the same job forever. Because there's certainly someone coming up behind you who is willing to learn this stuff and make an impression on senior management. Think the senior team doesn't want to hear your ideas on how to outflank your rivals? They don't have all the answers, you know, and they really like it when leaders at all levels keep one eye on the competition. In the end, do you think they'd rather promote the person who fully understands the big picture or the one who has an old pair of company blinders on? The fact is to be a valuable asset to the company, you need to take a holistic and current view of the marketplace. You need to have a comprehensive working knowledge of what's going on with your competitors. This isn't something that's "nice to do"; in today's competitive climate, this is a "must-do."

Make a commitment to add a strong working knowledge of your company's competitors to your leadership portfolio. Set a goal of impressing your peers and boss with a clear understanding of the challenges facing the company this year, relative to the competition. You'll be surprised at how good it feels to be the most knowledgable person at the table. Don't be the corporate ostrich who only knows its own company; get out there and learn about who's coming after you!

Bootstrap
Takeaways

Know Your Competitors

1. As a leader, you have a responsibility to learn as much as you can about the competition. Develop a comprehensive working knowledge of what business you're in and who else is in it with you.

2. Learn a few basic facts about your competitor's customers, financials, new products, and corporate climate.

3. Share this information with your team members, and challenge them to keep up to date on the competition, too. Make it a regular feature of your weekly staff meetings.

28

Go Back to School

Attend a Conference or Seminar

THEY SAY THE BEST THINGS in life are free. I think that's true of leadership self-development, too. Most of the ideas and techniques in this book don't come with a budget; they are simple things that will make a difference if you're serious about improving your leadership skills. The fact that they require you to plan and practice is rewarding in its own right; you're going to earn your growth as a leader, because you're the one putting in the work. But free only takes you so far, and sometimes it pays to invest in your development (or better yet, for your manager to invest). So load up your courage and walk into the boss's office—you're going to ask your boss to invest some dollars in his or her single best asset: you.

How should you spend this money? One of the best ways is to attend a conference or seminar in your area of expertise. I know, I know, you're going to scream "boondoggle" and say that's out of the question in this economy. But before you dismiss the idea, let's explore the value of this investment. We all know that leaders need to stay up-to-date on their technical or functional skills. If you don't have the credibility that comes with "knowing your stuff," it's hard to lead a group, especially any function where the technology or rules of the game change rapidly. How can you effectively lead a group of people if you don't know what they do or what they should be doing? Senior legal officers have to stay up on the latest regulations and laws; IT managers must stay current on new technology developments. Finance and HR leaders need to know the latest analysis and employment trends, respectively. Operations managers need to know about the latest production or manufacturing systems in their field. It's a fact of leadership: You need to stay current in your specific area of expertise or else you'll lose the team's respect (and your ability to lead). This is where the annual conference comes into play, because a conference is where the industry leaders and top vendors present the latest thinking and best practices. It's quite literally a feast of great ideas, and you can't afford to miss it.

When You Go, Get Into the Experience

Start by researching the best conferences to attend. Use the Web to identify the top choices in your field. After you narrow the list, consult your network to find out who attended the previous year. Find out what they thought of the quality of the sessions, presenters, and so forth, and ask if they'd go back. Finally, read the brochure carefully to make sure this is a must-attend conference. In other words, do your homework before requesting and spending the boss's money!

Once you've identified the right conference, start making the case to your boss. Share the brochure, and circle the sessions you're particularly interested in. Sell your attendance as something broader than just a few days in a sunny locale: Promise to bring home a great set of notes and present what you learn to your boss, your peers, and the broader team. If you do get the go-ahead to attend, go with a plan to become fully engaged. Don't use this as an opportunity simply to sit by the pool or go sight-seeing all day; that's a waste of money, and no one wins—least of all you. When you go, you need to take advantage of the full experience.

You need to attend all the sessions, take great notes, ask provocative questions, and do the networking. Here are four reasons why you should consider attending a conference or seminar this year:

1. **You'll learn something new.** Conferences provide a great platform for new research and surveys; there's a very good chance you'll be exposed to cutting-edge information you can use to build a business case or add credibility to your proposals. Much of what is presented at conferences is not yet published, so you can get a jump on the competition if you bring the research back and put it to good use. Talk to the presenters after the session; it's likely that they'll agree to send you a white paper or the full research results. This can be one of the best things you bring back to the company. Conferences that are known for presenting the latest research or survey findings are worth the price of admission.

2. **You'll bring home useful ideas.** Most conferences feature the "best practice" concept, where the top companies in the world present ideas that you might not have considered yet. I remember walking away from one of my first conferences with more ideas than we could implement (I'm sure I overwhelmed the team in my first few weeks after the event). Those three days left a big impression on me and changed the way I saw the field. Where else could I have gained access to the best companies in the world? A good conference will show you what "great" looks like. Pay attention and you can learn things that you can put to immediate use back on the job; and these ideas come with a stamp of approval, as these practices have been implemented in some of the best companies. It's particularly useful to learn what your competitors are doing, so try to identify conferences where they are presenting. Sharpen your pencil, and be prepared to take extensive notes.

3. **The networking is easy.** Do you find it difficult to meet people at other companies? These types of events make it easy for you; you're literally thrown together for two or three days, and if you don't meet five new colleagues in such a forum, then you're not trying hard enough. All you have to do is visit with people at lunch and at your tables in the sessions. Even if you don't prefer the cocktail reception or coffee break routines, it's easy to make new contacts by attending only the sessions. Talk to as many people as you can. Exchange business cards and then follow up twice a year with an email to stay in touch (apply the lessons from Chapter 23). Meet the "stars" in your industry, and add them to your contact list; who knows, you might be able to ask for their help in the future if you establish a connection at the conference. If you're naturally shy, I'd recommend you acknowledge that, and then set that trait aside for the week. Assume a new identify for two days; you can do it. Networking is essential if you want to take your leadership game to a new level, and conferences and seminars are a great place to practice your skills.

4. **You'll have time to reflect.** I have always found conferences to be a wonderful opportunity to get away from my day job and just think. Look at it as a chance to take a break from your regular duties to ponder some interesting questions and challenge your own thinking (use the template from Chapter 17). Spend your time at the conference wisely; there will be plenty of work waiting for you back at the office. This is a chance for you to spend a little time by yourself, absorbing new information and reflecting on how you can be even more effective.

Approached with the right attitude, conferences and seminars can be highly efficient resources on which to spend your development dollars. You can't beat them as a source of information or ideas, and you'll meet a lot of new people who are facing the same challenges as you. It's not free, that's true. But the payback is often worth the investment. Who knows, you might even have some fun, and what's not to like about that?

Bootstrap
Takeaways

Attend a Conference or Seminar

1. Sometimes you have to invest real dollars in your development; conferences and seminars can be great ways to spend that budget.
2. Attend the conference on a mission to learn as much as you can and meet as many new people as possible. If you have to, invent a new persona, but get into it. The payback is worth it.
3. Bring the education back to the job. Take great notes, and prepare and share a presentation with your team. Get an additional return on that investment by practicing your writing and speaking skills.

29

Road Trip!

Visit Innovative Companies

WHEN'S THE LAST TIME you got a really good look inside another company to see how its people do things or, better yet, how they reinvent themselves? When's the last time you saw a new process, a new piece of equipment, or a new service idea up close? Wouldn't it be useful to get a firsthand look at something that you could bring back and apply in your organization? And wouldn't it be valuable to give this gift to your team to spark their creativity and imagination? Chances are the last time you really knew how another company worked was when you were *at* that other company. Well, even your previous employer has probably changed quite a bit since you worked there; so you don't even really know what they're up to these days, do you?

This begs the question: How are you teaching your team the value of leveraging new ideas? Sure, you can read about other companies in the trade magazines and business press, and you can attend conferences and seminars to get a firsthand briefing about best practices (Chapter 28). And if you're doing these things on a regular basis, good for you—you're staying up to date in your chosen profession. But why not strive for a closer look? And why not take your team with you?

Innovation: The Job of Every Leader

Part of your job as a leader is to continually challenge your people to find a better way to get things done. Where possible, you should drive a mindset of change and new ideas. In short, you should demand innovation. The question you should repeatedly ask is: "How can we do things better, cheaper, faster?" Now, you can certainly develop many of your own ideas; after all, you know your processes and services better than anyone else. But sometimes it helps to see what others are doing, so you can iterate and adapt. That's why best practice benchmarking is so popular—if it's working over there, perhaps you can make it work over here. You know all this, of course, which is why you make time for brainstorming sessions, read about other companies, and encourage your team members to keep reinventing their work. But there's another way to spark innovation that turns the best practices game on it's head a bit—an exercise that allows you to build the team's collective exposure to innovation while giving them a unique learning experience at the same time. Think of it as an innovation road trip.

In Search of Innovation

Here's the idea: You and your team are going to visit several companies in your region for a day of "corporate sightseeing." That's right; you're going to spend the day in another company with a singular mission in mind: to learn as much as you can about how they innovate and create new ideas. And you're going to do some team-building in the process. Start by bringing your team together to introduce the plan and discuss what you most want to learn. There are two general approaches to the innovation road trip, and your first task is to decide which is right for your team.

The first approach involves "targeted best practices" where you identify specific companies that do things similar to what your group does, only better (or so you believe). The goal of this approach is to get a close look at how other companies go about doing the work that you most want to improve. You'll be on familiar ground here and should look for incremental ideas in order to evolve your process, products, or services. There's nothing wrong with this approach, although for obvious reasons, you'll have a difficult time accessing your direct competitors (where perhaps you most want do this type of research).

The second approach is purely an "open source" pursuit, and it is much more fun and adventurous. In this model, you and the team target local companies that are known to be creative and imaginative but that purposefully have nothing in common with your business. In fact, the more different they are from your company the better; the idea is to visit innovative organizations, regardless of what they do, make, or sell. For example, if you work in financial services, you might identify a museum, a ballet or theater company, a manufacturing plant, an advertising agency, or even a brewery (sign me up for that one)—any place where innovation is known to percolate and thrive. In this approach, you're not after the ideas themselves (although some may transfer); instead, your purpose is to learn *how* these organizations do innovation. Do they have a process? Is it in their DNA, and if so, how did they create and sustain that culture? Where do the ideas come from? How do they operationalize them? How do they reward teams or individuals for the ideas and their execution?

Ideally, gather twenty to twenty-five people for this outing. If your team isn't big enough, partner with a peer and do this as a joint project to bring your groups together and build relationships. Break the larger group into teams of four or five people, taking care to mix up your talent to fully leverage this shared experience. Then get them involved in picking the target companies, and ask for volunteers to reach out to make contact. Because you'll spend a full day at this company, try to schedule some of the following: a tour of the plant or facility, meetings with selected midlevel leaders, briefings with the R&D department, focus groups with employees, a look inside their customer service or data facilities, and so forth. Every hour of the day ought to be related in some way to their reputation as a product, process, or service innovator. You're there to learn "how they do it" and get a sense of what's in their culture that really makes it all come alive.

Coordinate the team's visits so they all happen on the same day. Meet in the conference room for a short briefing, and then send them out for what will surely *not* be a typical work day. Arm yourselves with the mission: to ask a lot of questions and bring back some new perspectives. And yes, you're going to travel with your team; in fact, it's a perfect opportunity to socialize with some of your extended team that you don't often spend time with (see Chapter 44). Be a role model and display the intellectual curiosity and optimism that this day requires. Afterward, you'll gain plenty of goodwill from spending a day with the troops, doing something that's new and different for *all* of you.

The next day, host the full group for some lively reporting of their findings. Use the entire day to listen in-depth to each other's discoveries and brainstorm what it all means for your department or company. How can you apply the learnings to your own work? What did you learn from this "perpendicular" look at other organizations? Let your team drive the day's agenda, and sit back and watch the light bulbs come on.

If you're looking for a fun, creative way to develop your team, plan an innovation road trip and turn everyone loose on a "scavenger hunt for new ideas." Put your own passion for innovation and development on display by carving out two full days for this team event, and give your people a unique learning opportunity they won't soon forget. The whole experience has the added benefit of potentially driving some important innovations for the company. You win all the way around—not only do you develop yourself but you also create a memorable learning experience for your team, one that just might result in some new, big ideas. That's worth the trip, don't you think?

Bootstrap
Takeaways

Visit Innovative Companies

1. Take the best practice search to a new level by splitting the team into small groups and arranging for them to visit local companies that are known to be innovators.

2. Pay attention to *how* these companies innovate. What can you learn and adapt from their processes?

3. Share and discuss the learnings, looking for common themes and possible applications back at your company.

30

Bring It Home

Learn Something New—Outside of Work

LEADERSHIP SELF-DEVELOPMENT feels good, but it's a lot of work, isn't it? Hopefully, you're integrating the development into your regular routine and practicing some of your new skills on the job. Maybe you've mastered a few new tricks already, and they're just part of your leadership style now. Or maybe you've become so good at delegation that you're actually making time in your day for more of these game-changing ideas—that would be ideal.

No matter how much progress you're making, it's time to introduce another way to develop yourself, which can pay surprising dividends for you as a leader even though it's not directly related to the job. In fact, this development doesn't even happen at work; it happens at home, where your enthusiasm for family, friends, hobbies, and other personal interests at least matches (or exceeds) your fervor for the job.

Here's the idea: Because you've developed such a devotion to improving yourself as a leader, it's time to extend that passion for self-development outside of work. It's time to delve into something that interests you, something that has nothing to do with your career. No one can or should be focused 100 percent of the time on his or her job; it's not healthy, and frankly, it's not much fun, either (there's a reason "work" is a four-letter word, you know). So this chapter is about finding something *outside* of work to develop; it's about bringing home that same zest for curiosity and self-improvement that you have on the job. Why? Because finding a new hobby or rekindling an old one can round you out, giving you a new perspective that you can channel back to your leadership development. Working on becoming a better parent or friend has implications for leading your team more effectively. Taking a course at the local community college can teach you things that you can apply back on the job. The idea is to expand your knowledge, skills, or interests into areas that have nothing to do with work, but that might have everything to do with broadening your outlook as a leader. In other words, what can you do off the job that can help you on the job? A hobby or a renewed personal commitment at home teaches you plenty about leadership. The only question you have to answer is: "What am I going to do to give myself that 'off-the-job' spark that will complement my on-the-job development?"

Choose Your Passion

Do you have a hobby or a personal interest that you've put on hold because you're too busy with work? Or do you have no life, because you've thrown everything into your job and career? If so, maybe you *need* a hobby! Leadership positions are demanding roles; leaders are mentally (and maybe physically) challenged all day at work. It helps to have an outlet that reenergizes the mind, body, and spirit. A hobby provides a release from the other things in your life; it's something you do alone or with other people you enjoy being around. In short, you love your hobby because it enriches you in some way; otherwise, you wouldn't devote the time and energy to it. If you have a hobby that you're actively engaged in, great; keep it up. If you've let your hobby slip because you're too busy with other things, take a few steps back toward it and see if it doesn't brighten your mood; reconnecting with a dormant hobby can be a refreshing experience. If you don't have a hobby, find something that you'd enjoy spending time doing. Develop an interest in something completely different than your job, and see what fresh ideas it might present for you at work.

So what can your hobby teach you about leadership development? Most people achieve a high level of expertise or knowledge about their particular hobby because they're keenly interested in the subject. They get good at it through practice, by dedicating the time to learn about and perfect the activity. This is exactly the model for improving leadership—deep interest in the subject, disciplined practice, and dedication to the craft. Look at your hobby through a self-development lens, and ask yourself the following three questions.

1. **"Why am I doing this?"** Make a detailed list of the reasons you love your hobby. Write down everything you can think of, and be descriptive.
2. **"How did I get good at this?"** Examine the pattern of discipline that allowed you to reach a high level of achievement in your passion. What did it take? Again, be specific.
3. **"What am I getting out of this?"** List the benefits you find from engaging with your hobby. What's in it for you? How are you and others rewarded for your dedication to this activity?

You can probably tell already why it helps to examine your hobbies in this way. Yes, these questions help you reflect *directly* on your hobby and your relationship with it, which is a pretty interesting exercise in its own right (you might be surprised at the depth of insight you gain from this self-analysis). But I want you to examine how your development of your hobby *parallels* your development as a leader. Ask yourself these same questions about your leadership role, and see if some of the same answers apply. Then reflect on what that means to you.

In my case, running was my passion. What I loved about it was the sense of accomplishment it gave me. I'd set a goal, achieve it, and aim higher the next time—just like leading my team to new and bigger objectives. How did I get better at running? Through sheer practice of course, but also by reading a lot about the subject, which helped me improve my technique, training methods, equipment, and so forth. The disciplined approach I took to studying running was something I began to apply to my development as a leader; I began to study the subject of leadership and to apply the learnings. Finally, in terms of what I was getting out of running, clearly fitness was at the top of the list, but it was more than that. Running gave me a high level of confidence and was a great source of new ideas. I'd come home with a new idea every time I went for a run. I realized that carving out time to think (there isn't much else to do while running!) produced results. I brought that lesson back to the job and started to spend at least thirty minutes a day in my office just thinking about things, searching for new ideas. By examining my hobby and looking for parallels to my "other" passion—developing myself into a better leader—I was able to marry the lessons from both pursuits, which made both endeavors more enjoyable.

While you're busy developing yourself as a leader, set aside time to become a more well-rounded person. Start (or keep) pursuing that passion outside of work, and use your hobbies as a metaphor for learning. Ask yourself why you're in it, how you got good at it, and what you're getting out of it. Then apply those lessons to your journey of self-development as a leader. By broadening your interests and your pursuit of excellence, you can gain useful insight that will help you become a better leader. Embrace your hobby as something that's more than just an outlet from everyday life; consider it complementary to your leadership development. But that's enough work for one day: Get out there and spend some time with your personal passion!

Bootstrap
Takeaways

Learn Something New—Outside of Work

1. Apply your discipline and passion for self-development outside of work. Pursue or find a hobby or personal interest.

2. Draw the parallels between what you love about your hobby and your journey of discovery as a leader. What stands out for you as you compare the two?

3. Share your passion with others—tell your team about your hobbies, and ask about theirs. Hobbies define us, and help others understand us. Share the why, how, and what of your hobby so people can relate to you.

Part Four

Step Out of Your Comfort Zone

ARE YOU READY for the next step in your development journey? By now, you have a good idea of the current leadership skills in which you need further development, and maybe you've already added a few new techniques to your toolkit. Perhaps you've found some new ways to stretch yourself beyond your current boundaries, as well. Now it's time to take more risks with your development; it's time to *really* step out of your Comfort Zone. In this section, you'll find suggestions and ideas that may seem familiar, because you've told yourself for years that you should try them. Deep down, you know you should be stepping out of your Comfort Zone, but you just can't seem to make it happen. Well, here's your chance—you've started down the path of creating a new leadership brand, so you might as well take the next step. All it takes is a little confidence and courage (which you're developing, yes?).

How about taking a more proactive stance with your boss about your next assignment or role? What if you become more aggressive about what *you* want to do next? What about joining that professional network in your city that meets once a month? C'mon, it's not *that* scary—you can do it! Oh, here's a common fear: public speaking. Would you rather do most anything other than speak to a large group of people? OK, so you share this fear with millions of others, but don't you think it's time to overcome it? Does making presentations to senior management make you nervous? Better add that to the list of things you need to master if you're going to move up in the organization. Do you have trouble admitting mistakes, or seeing things from another perspective? Perhaps you should work on that, too, if you have dreams of advancement. How about admitting that you don't know everything there is to know about how your organization really works, or how it makes money?

We all have certain fears as a leader, and we've worked around them for years. But if you truly want to break out and move up, you need to take your development to a whole new level. Challenge yourself with some of these suggestions; it might be your most rewarding project yet.

31

Get Outside the Circle

Practice New Leadership Behaviors

BELIEVE IT OR NOT, you've built an invisible circle around yourself over the years. And subconsciously, you protect and even nurture this circle—it's called your Comfort Zone. Don't worry, we all have them, in our personal *and* professional lives. The Comfort Zone is where all of your favorite beliefs, attitudes, and behaviors flourish. The Comfort Zone is where you feel confident, calm, and self-assured. It is where the person that you (and others) recognize feels comfortable. This is your safe space, where you operate from a familiar style.

But you've actually been testing your Comfort Zone, haven't you? How's it feel to be stepping outside the circle? As you've been stretching and challenging yourself to be a better leader, what are you noticing when you're outside the Zone? Do words such as unsettled, panicky, tense, uneasy, and uncomfortable come to mind? This is natural, too; as it turns out, pulling yourself up by your own bootstraps is hard work. It *feels* strange, and it should; you're stepping outside your known world—and the unknown is often scary. But I hope you're also feeling excited, creative, energized, renewed, and open-minded. Because here's the little secret about Comfort Zones: It's only when you step outside the Zone that you learn, grow, and develop (see Figure 6). Learning happens best when you're pushed out of your Comfort Zone. If there's an overall theme to draw from this book, it's that you have to feel a little discomfort to produce meaningful and lasting change. You have to expand and push yourself out of your Comfort Zone in order to grow as a leader.

So let's go back to the beliefs, attitudes, and behavior patterns that you've had for years—let's collectively call them "your way." You've no doubt cultivated and nurtured your way of doing things; it's become your unique style of thinking, acting, and speaking. You're not only comfortable with your way of doing things, you may actually believe it's the *only* way to operate. You have a comfortable way of starting your day, a habit of eating lunch with the same people, even a certain way of responding to your boss. Am I right? Does this sound familiar? You're in your Comfort Zone, and if you're like most people, you're very happy there.

But what would happen if you stepped outside the circle more often? What opens up if you let in some new thoughts, adopt a new attitude, or start doing things differently? We've already explored the value of looking at your thoughts from another angle (Chapter 9) and allowing your attitudes to be altered by other cultural norms (Chapter 21). This chapter explores the idea of experimenting with some new behaviors. Are you ready to start doing some of the same old tasks or routines a little differently? Variety is the spice of life and trying out new leadership behaviors is a great way to expand your repertoire of leadership skills.

Let's say you've always set goals with your direct reports the same way. You give them an assignment or a task to do, tell them when you need it, and tell them (within certain parameters) how you want it done. What if you turn that around, and allow them to select and identify the projects? If that's not possible, how about allowing them to flesh out the assignment in terms of details and deadlines? The point is to experiment with different ways of assigning and monitoring the work.

How about the way you run your staff meeting? Pretty much the same every week, isn't it? It may be effective and productive (although if it's not, you should definitely change it up!), but what can you unlock in terms of creativity and imagination if you conducted the meeting in other ways? Start by sitting in a different chair at the table, or have the meeting last forty-five minutes instead of an hour. Change the venue or the day of the week. If you use a lot of pre-reading, try doing the meeting without any material. If you don't use pre-reads, send out a deck in advance for people to review. If you normally run the meeting, let a direct report manage the process. If you always go around the room for updates, try addressing just one or two issues as a group, instead. The idea is to try out some new leadership behaviors and see what happens.

Another common "routine" leaders may find themselves in is the way they respond to the boss. Your boss knows your particular buttons and knows how you're likely to respond to just about any scenario. Are you happy with that level of predictability? What if you did something to alter the relationship? I distinctly remember a boss who had a habit of giving me assignments just as I was getting ready to go home for the day. I dutifully took the work home and had it completed by the next morning, only to watch him leave it on his desk until mid-afternoon or even the next day. One night, as he assigned me something to do, I told him in a calm voice that I would add this to my immediate workload and would have it for him by 2 p.m. the next day. He clearly picked up on my underlying message but didn't say anything, and I did the work the next morning when I came in. I took a risk and changed the routine, and it worked; I took back control of my evenings.

Here's another boss story. One of my managers had a habit of calling me out of a meeting if he wanted to talk to me. Essentially, I had to be available at any time to take a call from this guy. For the most part, I was OK with this, especially if it involved an emergency. But it happened once when I was doing a performance appraisal with one of my direct reports, and so I had a very clear discussion with the boss about it afterward. I told him that I wouldn't take that call again under those circumstances—it had interrupted the flow of a difficult conversation, and I thought it was completely unnecessary and insensitive to the employee. Sure enough, it happened again about a week later, and I told my admin to tell the boss I was unavailable to take his call. After the performance appraisal meeting, I called the boss to check in. He wasn't happy, but I had stood my ground and altered a small part of our relationship. I'd like to think I gained some respect from the boss that day by standing on principle (especially because it reinforced our official company values). However, I would never have gotten this result if I hadn't stepped outside my Comfort Zone.

The key lesson of the Comfort Zone is that when you want a different result, you have to do something different. You have to take a chance and try something new, because your Comfort Zone is both a blessing and a curse. Yes, it helps you navigate this crazy world with some familiar routines and patterns and allows you to fit into your present environment. But it doesn't help you stretch and grow; in fact, it's specifically designed to prevent you from developing. If you want to change something about your beliefs, attitudes, or behaviors, make a conscious trip outside the circle— that's where you'll experience the adventure of learning. Search for ways to think, feel, or do things differently. Step out of your Comfort Zone and open yourself to new ways of looking at the world. It may be the biggest leap you'll take along this path of self-development.

Bootstrap
Takeaways

Practice New Leadership Behaviors

1. You don't have all the answers, and there are many ways to do things. Step out of your Comfort Zone and try some new leadership behaviors.

2. Encourage others to do things their way. Your Comfort Zone may be restricting your ability to empower your employees.

3. Ask others for feedback about your Comfort Zone. If they say you have an opportunity to branch out, practice some new ways of leading the team.

32

You're Right and I'm Wrong

Admit Mistakes and Limitations

ONE OF THE SECRETS to great leadership is balancing self-confidence and humility. Obviously, you need to have talent to be a great leader. You need to have the experience, drive, and opportunity to make big things happen. And every leader needs a certain degree of confidence (otherwise, others will quickly lose faith). But some leaders go off the rails because they can't control their confidence; when it's so off the charts that it turns into arrogance, greed, or recklessness, it becomes a liability. You have to balance self-confidence with humility. You have to remember that you don't have all the answers, and even if you do, you shouldn't act like you do. Nobody likes to work for someone who projects that kind of arrogance.

So how do you develop humility? Well, there's a good argument to be made that you're born with this trait. In many ways, you either have it or you don't. But that discussion is beyond the scope of this book. Let's focus here on ways you *can* cultivate modesty and humility. A truly great leader needs this quality, so it's important to pay attention to this aspect of your leadership style. Here are three ways to work on adding more humility to your game.

Develop Your Sense of Inclusion

First, ask others for their opinions on a regular basis. Then, more important, listen carefully to what they have to say. Great leaders seek answers from those around them. They never fail to gather opinions and suggestions from trusted advisors. Ask yourself: "Do I regularly ask others for their thoughts on matters of strategy, planning, or operations, and do I factor those opinions into my final decisions?" If the answer is yes, that's great—you're an inclusive leader. If the answer is no, well, I have some bad news for you. Your people don't enjoy working for you. Yes, that's right; the absence of this one behavior says, "I know best and will make all decisions unilaterally," and it guarantees you a spot in the ABHOF: the Awful Boss Hall of Fame. Think back to a time when you worked for a manager who never asked for your opinion and made all of the decisions without including you or your peers. Have a lot of good times with that boss, did you? Of course not. So if this sounds like you, the first thing you have to do is to ask others for their best thinking—early and often. Make this a permanent part of your leadership; it's actually very easy to do. Every time a major decision comes along, ask a few peers or direct reports one or more of the following questions: "How would you assess the risks here?" "What pros and cons do you see in this situation?" "How can we best leverage this situation?" "What are some of the implications of not making this decision?" Simply put, if a decision or action is required, seek some input. It's not hard to remember and not hard to do.

Humility: The Last Best Leadership Trait

For many leaders, humility is often the last leadership trait to fully develop; for some, it comes the hard way, through a huge mistake. Don't wait to learn humility from a critical incident. The second great way to develop this key leadership skill is to admit when you're wrong. If you're on the losing side of a debate, or just have the wrong answer on something, say so. Again, you're in a leadership position, which means you're a role model. Don't dig in your heels, hold your breath, or pout about it. You can't afford to be a jerk; others will think its OK to be a jerk, too. When you're wrong, simply admit it. Learn this phrase, and use it often: "You know what, you're right; I wasn't looking at this from all sides, and I see now that my approach isn't the best way to go." That's not so hard, is it? Yet a lot of leaders don't do it; they have difficulty saying, "You were right; I was wrong." That's unfortunate because these simple words have great value. It's not even an apology really; it's more of an acknowledgement of how much you value independent thinking. It's a way to express your gratitude that someone else has done his or her homework, or sees things more clearly, or simply has a better idea. Try this—it works. It disarms all kinds of situations and makes you look mature and open-minded. Besides, who wants to be right all the time? And if you are right all the time, you're probably not taking enough risks, which leaders need to do from time to time.

The third way to develop humility goes way back to what your parents taught you: When you've done something bad or been rude to someone, apologize. It's called being reasonable, polite, and well-mannered. Don't just say you're sorry, flesh it out a bit and be sincere. If you've been rude to someone in a staff meeting, tell them: "I'm sorry I cut you off a few times today. It's not professional of me to jump in before you finish speaking; I need to do a better job of letting you finish your thoughts, and I'm going to work on that." That's more specific and sincere than a half-hearted, "Hey, sorry I interrupted you a few times today."

Webster's Dictionary defines humility as: "the quality or condition of being humble; of having a modest opinion or estimate of one's own importance, rank, etc." That's really it, isn't it? Humble leaders don't think of themselves as being any more important than anyone else in the organization. In fact, they see themselves more as the conductor of the orchestra: They don't make any of the actual music; that work is done by the other members of the team. Take your leadership to the next level. Add a dash of humility to your skill set and then pay attention to how others respond to you. Trust me, they'll appreciate it and you'll certainly notice a difference.

Bootstrap
Takeaways

Admit Mistakes and Limitations

1. Practice humility. Make a conscious effort to take some of the shine off your leadership trophies—you didn't score all those points yourself.

2. Make asking others for their opinions and suggestions a regular part of your leadership style.

3. Remember that you're a role model. Be polite, say you're sorry when appropriate, and don't be afraid to say you were wrong once in an awhile—people gravitate toward humble leaders.

33

Become a Member

Join a Professional Network

HERE'S SOME ADVICE I bet you've never heard: Limit your network; don't create too many business relationships. The reason you've never heard this advice is because it's ridiculous. The fact is you *can't* have too many relationships. That's the beauty of networking: The process of adding new people to your contacts list is endless, and the importance of refreshing and renewing relationships with colleagues already in your network is constant (see Chapter 23). Well, there's one proven way to keep meeting new people, but it seems as though 90 percent of leaders completely ignore it—which is too bad, because it's an easy way to augment your development. Yes, I'm talking about joining a local networking or affiliate group (see, you're in that 90 percent, aren't you? I heard that groan).

How easy is this? You sign up, you go to a meeting once a month or maybe six times a year, you listen to a speaker and . . . here it comes, wait for it . . . you meet new people! Amazing! There are actually people out there who do exactly what you do! Yeah, there's nothing you can learn or gain from meeting and talking with other people in your field or discipline. That would be ridiculous, right?

What's Your Excuse?

I know you've got them: excuses. Heck, I had them for years, too. Let's explore the big four, shall we? First, you're too busy (an oldie but a goodie). Oh, I see . . . you're so good at delegating and empowering your staff that you're still working sixty hours a week. Second, it cuts into your personal time (this was my favorite). If they just had these things in the middle of the day, you'd be glad to take off work to attend; but many of the meetings are at night, when you need to be somewhere else. Third (and this one is more common than you might think), you're just too senior for that group. It would be a waste of your time to hang out with the people who attend those meetings. A variation on this theme is: "I just don't see the value." (But how would you know? You haven't been to any of the meetings!) Finally, you might be so incredibly shy that it makes you physically ill to think about mingling with a group of strangers. You know you should try, but you just can't make yourself join and attend. So, which of these is it for you? Because I know it's one of those.

Getting Your Head Around It

Let's back up for a minute. We have established that one way for you to develop yourself is to build a stronger network, yes? And we've agreed that this is important to your career, right? OK, good; I just wanted to be sure we are on the same page. Trust me, this is one of the things you need to do to grow and expand your skills. It's not that difficult—you can do it. Oftentimes, the hardest part is just getting your head around the *idea* of joining a network group. Once you decide to do it, the rest falls into place.

Whether you are in a big city or a small town, formal groups or networks abound. There are at least three types that you can join. The first type is the local chapter of a national group or network in your area of expertise. For me, it is some kind of HR group or OD (Organization Development) network. Typically, there is a monthly meeting, with a speaker and lots of "meet and greet" time with other members (we'll discuss how you can master the old "link and clink" in a moment). There are groups out there for every discipline, including HR, IT, Legal, Marketing, Operations, Risk, Compliance, Finance, and so on. These groups specialize in bringing the latest ideas and information to their members in compelling ways. You could benefit from that, right?

The second type is a general business group that focuses more on connecting leaders from the community (such as the Chamber of Commerce). Here, you might focus your time on local business issues, and you're certain to meet a wide variety of business leaders.

Third, your city might have an "emerging leaders" type of program or network that you can join. These are typically extended programs where you come together with leaders from other companies to form a cohort that focuses on developing leadership skills.

OK, I'm sure you know that these groups exist. And you know you're *supposed* to be using them to network. But how do you get out of your old mindset and make these groups work for you?

Push Past the Excuses

First, use the Internet to find the right groups for you (see Chapter 24). Be sure to locate a group that actually meets in person (you need the practice of talking face-to-face with new people). Once you've identified groups of interest, contact the administrator and ask a few questions. Find out when, where, and how often they meet. Ask about the membership: Who typically attends? Ask about the expectations: Can you just attend a meeting, or do you need to be actively involved? Ask about their last several speakers: What's the quality of the learning? Ask for the contact information of a few current members so you can find out what they think of the group (this also gives you a few people you can walk right up to at the first meeting). In short, do your homework, especially if you have choices. Second, talk to your boss about the benefits of joining so you can get the funding for it. State your case and pledge to be an active participant. Most companies will support this development opportunity if they can see a return on their investment (which might involve you bringing back information to a broader internal audience). Third, show up. That's right; you actually have to go to the meeting!

OK, so you've joined, you've made the commitment to your boss, and you're at the meeting. Now what? Start by setting a goal of meeting just one new person—that's right, only one new contact. You'll easily exceed this number, but that sets the bar low enough for even the most introverted among us. I know the cocktail party atmosphere can be intimidating; I sweated all the way through my first experience in college. But I've gotten better at it, and I'll tell you my secret. I wade into the crowd and find someone else who is standing alone (as opposed to joining a small circle of people already talking—that *is* awkward) and I simply say: "Hello, I'm Steve. What's your name?" Then, I focus all of my energy on learning who that person is and what that person does. I don't worry about getting to my story; if asked, I'll share it, but mostly I'm in question-and-listening mode. It's a lot easier (and more interesting) to listen to someone else than it is to carry the conversation; after all, you already know all about you. Try this and within two minutes you can accomplish your goal for the meeting; repeat this several times before the speaker begins and you'll well exceed your goal and feel great. The trick is to see the "meet and greet" portion of the meeting as a simple objective, with an emphasis on the "meet someone new" part of the game.

Finally, it can be very rewarding to serve on a committee or even the group's board. Talk about polishing your leadership skills in a different venue! Once you've been in the group awhile, look for opportunities to move into a leadership role. This is a way for you to "give back" to your field or community, and it's a great way to practice your strategic thinking, influencing, and of course, networking skills.

If meeting new people or navigating a cocktail reception is a challenge for you, think about joining a local networking group. The reassuring thing is that you already have a lot in common with the other members, so there's plenty to talk about. Don't hide behind the same old excuses. If your company is willing to pay the dues, you owe it to yourself to give this development opportunity a try. I know you've thought about it, so make the effort. Step out of your Comfort Zone, join a group, and start building that fabulous network, one relationship at a time.

Bootstrap
Takeaways

Join a Professional Network

1. Make the decision to join a networking group—that's the hardest part. It's the right thing to do for your career.
2. Look at these events as learning experiences—ask people questions. You'll develop your listening skills, learn something new, and add new people to your network.
3. Don't get too comfortable in your own role and company. There's a big world out there, and you can't absorb it from your office. Get out there!

34

Share Your Story

Organize an Internal Speaker's Bureau

ARE YOU GETTING THE HANG of this leadership thing yet? How are your people feeling? Are they engaged, motivated, ready to take on the next challenge? Is everyone empowered, working on the right big things? What about you? Do you feel good about your strategy? Is the boss satisfied with where things are? Do you feel like you're adding value and making all the right moves? Yes? Good! Because if that's the case, if everything is good at home, it's time for an "inside the company" road trip. That's right—you're ready to take this act on the road, my friend. Don't worry, you don't need to ask the boss to boost your expense account because you don't need to leave town; you probably won't even leave the building because this is a different kind of road trip, although one that has you very much in the driver's seat. You see, you're going to take your team's *story* on the road, to other departments around the company. And you're going to create a way for others to follow your lead, too.

Double Your Development

Your team is doing great: You've got the right strategy, everyone's working hard, you're moving the ball forward. But has anyone noticed? Does the organization really know what your group does? Let's say you're in a line function, where the money's made. Wouldn't it be great if everyone in the organization had a good working knowledge of how your team interacts with suppliers, partners, and customers? Is it worthwhile to have different departments around the company understand how your team supports the organization? The answer is yes on both counts. And that's where you come in. Are you ready to lead beyond your own team? Are you ready to do something to remedy the lack of knowledge of what everyone's doing across the company? An easy way to make everyone smarter about the organization is to create an internal speaker's bureau. That's right, not only are you going to take your story to other departments, but you're also going to organize the whole process of executives sharing their stories across the company. You'll develop your speaking prowess *and* your networking skills, while providing a valuable service for the organization. What do you say—are you game?

First, make a list of all the departments in the organization. List any group that makes a significant impact on the business. Then, invite one leader from each of these teams to a meeting (yes, we'll forgive you this one bureaucratic meeting) where you will lay out your plans for the speaker's bureau. The key here is that the representatives from each department don't need to be top leaders; in fact, it's a better development exercise if they're not. If you really want to emphasize this idea, ask HR to recommend the leaders in each department who most *need* public speaking experience. That way, you can be responsible for several leaders' self-development in addition to your own.

Next, because most departments have all-hands or expanded leadership team meetings periodically throughout the year, target these events for your internal "concert tour" of speakers. Suggest a loose format for the presentations, so audiences can get used to the same rhythm. A flow that works well is:

1. **Who are you?** Share your organizational chart and the key players' roles.
2. **What do you do?** Present your vision, mission, and strategy.
3. **How are you doing?** Show your goals and objectives for the year and progress to date.

Recommend that your speakers spend about forty minutes with slides or other multimedia presentations, and leave twenty minutes for Q&A. Encourage creativity, and suggest the leaders have some fun with this activity. After you've recruited the participants, it's time to build the master calendar. This is where you become an amateur booking agent as you match leaders to speaking engagements. The goal is to have every major group in the organization hear from at least four leaders throughout the year. If you map it correctly, you'll find plenty of opportunities for leaders to tell their stories, spreading the word of how their teams serve customers or other functions in the company.

I've seen this work, and it does have the desired impact. At my last company, about every eight weeks, a leader from another part of the organization spoke to the HR department. Everyone agreed they gained a much better understanding of what the featured group did after these sessions. We also learned about the group's leaders, what their unique challenges were, and sometimes, how we could leverage that team to help us accomplish *our* objectives. The experience was worthwhile and required little effort on our part: A tailored presentation about another aspect of the organization was brought right to our doorstep and we only had to listen and engage.

I was one of the leaders who traveled around the company telling my team's story. My team had just founded the new corporate university, so this gave me an opportunity to market our programs, answer questions, and generally get people interested in formal learning. My team helped to build the presentation (a good team exercise in its own right), and I acquired much-needed confidence as a public speaker over the course of several speeches. I also used this program as an opportunity to meet a lot of new people across the company and build my network.

You can do this too, no matter how small or large your organization. Even if you just get "on the road" yourself, this can be a valuable learning experience. Craft a story, and volunteer to share it with groups around the company. If you're ambitious and have the time, take the idea to a larger stage. Identify departments you know others would be interested in, and persuade leaders in these groups to participate. Then start brokering speaking opportunities across the company. If you set your mind to this, you can develop your own skills as a speaker, share your team's story, meet a lot of fellow leaders, and most important, be responsible for knitting the organization together. That last item is a worthy objective indeed. Who would have thought that by developing your own leadership skills, you can actually raise the level of working knowledge and awareness across the entire company? Pretty cool, huh?

Bootstrap
Takeaways

Organize an Internal Speaker's Bureau

1. Take charge of your own public speaking skills development—create a presentation about your team's contributions and share it with other groups inside the company.
2. Recruit other leaders inside the company to join you, and set up an internal speaker's bureau.
3. Broker the match between speakers and audience, working to build awareness of what different departments do across the company.

35

Tell the Boss You're Bored

Take Charge of Your Own Career

LET'S FACE IT: You need your boss. Unless you work for yourself, the boss is still an organizational necessity and is a major part of your work experience. Your boss hands out work assignments, makes sure you get paid, keeps you from falling asleep in meetings, and hopefully protects you when you make a mistake. But sometimes the boss is the last to notice when you're ready for something new. This is understandable. After all, the boss is focused on making the team look good (not to mention him- or herself) and that can be a full-time job. No, it's your job to manage your boss, and that includes communicating when you're ready for something else, such as a new project or assignment or even a new job somewhere else in the company.

Now, you can't just walk in and say "I want to do something different," prior to meeting certain criteria. First, a great performance record is a must-have for this discussion; you better be knocking the ball out of the park or else your boss will laugh you out of the office when you ask for a bigger, better role. Results come first, no matter how large or small the role or organization. It also helps to have a sense of the culture and how things work around your company. If you've only been in your role for a year, and the unwritten code is that managers need to "pay their dues," well, you better factor that into your thinking. It's probably going to be an issue.

Second, you must bring a plan with you. Do your homework so that you have an idea of what you want and a few reasons why this is such a brilliant idea. You need to sell yourself and your proposal, and you better be prepared to answer your boss's questions. If you want to expand your role, why do you think you can take on more team members or responsibility? If you propose that you move to a new position, who is available to replace you? Why is this the right time to make this move? What are your long-term career goals? Think through both sides of the conversation; anticipate what your boss is likely to say, feel, and do, and be ready with your responses. Prepare to defend your position, and try to steer the conversation toward why this is good for you *and* the company.

Sell Your Strengths and Make Your Case

Let's say you're a high performer, and you feel you could make a greater contribution. Or maybe you've learned everything you can in your current role. Congratulations, you've reached Step 1: realizing your strengths and identifying what motivates you. Write it down, and be prepared to articulate your unique skills and desired contribution to the boss (see Chapter 7). Boredom is not a virtue; if you've proven yourself and have capabilities that are being unused in your current role, it's time to speak up. Pair this with grateful appreciation for what your boss has already done for you. The conversation might go something like this: "I really appreciate what you've done to help me learn my current job. I'm enjoying it very much, but I'd like to explore taking on more responsibility/trying something new." Follow that with your thoughtful self-assessment and specific ideas: "I think I'm pretty

good at X, and I'd really like the opportunity to take on/explore/
work on Y." You've just done half the work by expressing appreciation and firmly stating your case. Now prepare for Step 2: bringing suggestions to the table.

Lay out your ideal next job and the reasons why it makes sense.
Maybe it's expanding your current role or shedding some of what
you do to focus on a specific task. Maybe it's moving up in your
current department to a leadership position just above your current role. Or maybe it's an entirely new job elsewhere in the organization. Whatever it is, have your facts straight and a strong
rationale for your reasoning. A helpful resource to consult as you
prepare for this discussion is *The Lessons of Experience,* which
makes the case for career development from a "learning by doing"
perspective.[15] Read this book, and you'll be prepared to say: "Here's
why I think this is good for me and the team/company." Be firm,
but don't back your boss into a corner. The secret is to ask for your
boss's input and support in helping you achieve your goals. After
expressing what you'd like to do, say: "I'd like to get your thoughts
on this; what do you think?" And as the conversation goes along,
don't be afraid to ask directly for support. Say: "Can you help me
make this happen?" or "Is there anything else you need from me?"

Your immediate boss is probably the most important person in
your work life, certainly as far as advancing your career is concerned. Each boss you work for has the power to help you move
forward and accelerate your career or frankly, derail it. Don't be
that manager who sits in the same job year after year waiting for
the boss to offer a new and exciting role. Pull yourself up by your
own bootstraps, and go out and make the case for yourself. If you
don't do it, who will? Do you really want to risk putting your career in someone else's hands? Make your boss an offer, present it
with passion and conviction, and appeal to your boss's sense of
pride in helping you move your career forward. If you've nailed

your current role, chances are good that your boss will be there for you. Just don't be afraid to have the conversation!

Bootstrap
Takeaways

Take Charge of Your Own Career

1. Be proactive and assertive about your career moves—don't be afraid to ask for your next assignment (once you've mastered the current one).

2. Let your boss know that you're interested in your next role—don't make your boss guess. Have a plan, and be prepared to sell yourself!

3. Seek out a role that best suits your skills and future learning objectives—think of jobs in terms of what they can teach you.

36

Love the Numbers

Learn to Read Financial Statements

HERE'S A RIDDLE: What's one aspect of leadership that some leaders absolutely love, some leaders hate, yet most leaders don't know how to do properly? The answer is: reading financial statements! Which camp are you in? If you're in Finance, you love financial statements, don't you? This is your business; it's how you keep score, right? Then there are the lines of business leaders who really hate to look at these statements in bad times because they're full of some pretty ugly news. Yet most leaders don't even know how to read financial statements, so they simply avoid them. I'm not referring to your department's budget—that's not that hard to read (even though it's frequently outdated or just plain wrong, but that's between you and the Finance group). No, I'm talking about the big statements, the ones that make it into the annual report. Have you read any good financial statements lately? I didn't think so. That's OK, you can admit it—you can confess that you've let this skill slide all these years. But here's a tip: If you want to keep moving your career forward, you need to add this missing link to your leadership chain. You want to *really* step out of your Comfort Zone? Then tackle this particular development challenge; it will pay big dividends for you in the future.

Four Statements on Your Must-Read List

There are four main financial statements that most companies prepare and report. These include: 1) the balance sheet, 2) the income statement, 3) cash flow statements, and 4) statements of shareholders' equity. Sometimes these are referred to by different names, but these are the basic statements. Let's take a look at each one briefly—a sort of "crash course" in reading financial statements.

The balance sheet shows what the company owns (assets) and what it owes (liabilities) at a fixed point in time. Assets include physical property, such as equipment, facilities, and inventory, in addition to things that can't be touched but nevertheless exist and have value, such as trademarks and patents. Liabilities are amounts of money that a company owes to others and can include all kinds of obligations, such as rent, loans, payroll, money owed for materials or goods, and taxes owed to the government. The statement of shareholder equity is included in the balance sheet and is sometimes called net worth or capital. It's the money that would be left if a company were to sell all of its assets and pay off all of its liabilities. So, essentially the balance sheet shows the "balance" between assets on the one hand and liabilities and shareholder equity on the other (hopefully, there's a positive number on that shareholder equity line!).

The income statement shows how much money a company made and spent over a specific period of time (usually a year). This is where you'll find revenues and expenses—the net of which (the literal "bottom line") is the company's net earnings or losses. The income statement tells you how much the company made or lost in the time period. Income statements typically report earnings per share (EPS) data, too. This tells you how much money shareholders would receive if the company were to distribute all of its net earnings for the period (which almost never happens, of course). To calculate EPS, take the total net income and divide it by the number of outstanding shares of the company.

Cash flow statements show the exchange of money between a company and other businesses or institutions over a period of time. This is an important statement (especially lately) because companies need to have enough cash on hand to pay expenses, purchase assets, and so forth. This statement is often a good barometer of a company's true health.

That's a start, but of course there is much more to learn. There are dozens of financial terms that you probably hear every day but may not be familiar with (depreciation, amortization, charges, write-offs, etc.). Some of them are mysterious, but others you should know in order to effectively talk finance with the top leaders in the company. Which brings us to your development task: How are you going to get up to speed on reading, understanding, and interpreting financial statements?

One easy way, of course, is to self-teach. Buy a book or do some online research, and try to put the pieces together on your own. If you choose this route, good luck—but don't read the book right before going to bed, or you'll be reading one page at a time for years. There's no doubt you'll find what you need, but if you haven't been motivated to self-teach by now, you may want to consider a different approach to this task. A better strategy might be to take a Finance colleague to lunch and beg him or her to tutor you on the basics of reading financial statements (it's a great way to expand your network inside the company, too). Seriously though, go to the source and ask for some guidance or lessons. Trust me, like everyone else, Finance people love to talk about their world, they have plenty of examples lying around, and they'll be happy to teach you what you want to know. Finally, see if your corporate learning center or local community college has the classic "finance for non-financial managers" course. If not, look into taking a three- to five-day course from a university or training outfit. Variations of the "non-financial managers" theme have been taught for at least fifty years, and most will meet your needs. Such courses are designed to explore the details of reading financial statements and are usually reasonably priced.

The point is that financial statements aren't just for Finance leaders. If you want to be taken seriously as a true "business leader," you need to have at least a working knowledge of balance sheets, income statements, and cash flow. You need to be able to hold you own in a conversation about how the company's doing financially. You need to be able to listen in to the quarterly earnings call (another good way to learn about finance) and clearly comprehend what the CEO tells the analysts. In short, you need to get your head in the game, and the game of business is money. Learn to love the numbers, and you can cross that particular blind spot off your development list!

Bootstrap
Takeaways

Learn to Read Financial Statements

1. You need to know your way around corporate financial statements. Don't put this off any longer—make learning to read these reports a priority.
2. There are only a few basic statements you need to learn—ask your Finance group to point you in the right direction.
3. Add this knowledge to your skills set—you won't go any higher without being able to talk intelligently about finance.

37

Build the Business Case

Give Great Presentations

ONE OF THE MOST IMPORTANT skills you can develop as a leader is your ability to influence others. In fact, it might be the single best determinant of your standing in the organization—you either have influence (with the right people) or you don't. If you're successfully influencing others, it means that they find you credible, believe your data, and trust your judgment. You get to weigh in on important decisions and push your agenda with peers and senior leaders. It doesn't get any better than that. If you have broad influence across your organization, congratulations; you've clearly earned it, because being recognized as an influencer isn't something that's handed out to just anyone. If you're trying to *establish* your reputation as an influencer, keep at it; it's definitely something you want to achieve as a leader.

Whether you already are an influencer or are striving to reach that level, be warned: Influence is one of those things that you can lose, too. There's nothing worse than being accepted into the "inner circle" but then, for some reason, being excluded from particular discussions or decisions. It can leave you scratching your head. What happened? How did you go from being asked for your opinion or having your suggestions praised to being on the outside looking in? This chapter explores ways to boost your influencing skills and achieve, maintain, or recapture your status as a trusted resource for decisions. In order to move up in the company, you're going to need to influence others—a lot.

Know the Influencing Landscape

The first thing you need to know about influencing others is that people have different influencing preferences. That is, some leaders are influenced by data or facts, whereas others respond emotionally to impassioned pleas or "gut" arguments. Try to use an influencing style that doesn't fit your intended target's preferred style, and you'll strike out every time. This happened to me early in my career as I struggled to influence the COO about a leadership development program I wanted to launch. I needed his support, but I wasn't getting anywhere, even after repeated meetings. Why? I was trying to influence him by the power of my brilliant arguments; I was demonstrating passion, but I was relying completely on a "trust me, I'm the expert" style. I thought that was all I needed to do—couldn't he see that I was on the right track? At one point, I even said: "Don't you see how great this will be?" Whoops. My mistake was not realizing that the COO made decisions based *only* on facts, logic, and data. He had to see it in black and white to be convinced of its value. Fortunately, his chief of staff took me aside and coached me on how to approach him using his preferred style. I built a business case for the project, presented it to him with retention, engagement, and succession planning data, and eventually got him to sign on as a sponsor of the program. In the end, I had to match my approach to the COO's preferred style. I've never forgotten this lesson and have tried ever since to learn what my boss expects when it comes to influencing his or her decision making. So, do your homework: Know what your leaders are looking for and what moves them. Generally, data is the great equalizer; bringing a business case or some facts to the party almost never fails. Usually, you'll at least get your foot in the door. But if you rely on the "trust me, I know what I'm doing" approach, chances are you'll have trouble influencing consistently across the organization.

Build Your Case

One of the best ways to build your business case is with a Power-Point presentation, which seems to be the influencing tool of choice in organizations today. An advantage to committing your case to paper is that it can potentially influence others even if you're not there to present it in person (although this is preferable, of course). PowerPoint draws a lot of criticism, but it can be a very effective means to present your case and fuel your influencing effort. The trick is to keep your presentation brief, get to the main points quickly, and leave plenty of time for discussion, questions, and some of that passion and personal gravitas (yes, after you present the data, you can close the deal with your winning personality). If you want to try a minimalist approach to building a presentation, use the following model of a business case that requires only five PowerPoint slides.

Slide 1: The Issue You're Trying to Solve. Start with the problem you're trying to solve. Acknowledge the issue at hand, complete with any supporting data that makes it critical or time-sensitive. This serves to focus your audience on what you're going to talk about and why it's important.

Slide 2: The Solution, Answer, or Approach. Don't bury the lead any longer; your next slide should include your plans to solve the issue. This is the slide you'll spend the most time on—it is your money slide. This is where you'll likely field the most questions, too, so be prepared. Know your facts, and be objective about the plan; don't become overly defensive about it if pushed. A useful technique is to include three options on this slide, with a clear indication of which one you recommend. This shows you're open to different ways of solving the problem but also demonstrates your decisiveness.

Slide 3: Supporting Evidence. Next, add a slide of supporting data or evidence to indicate why this approach is the preferred solution.

Slide 4: Budget, Resources, and Time Frames. Your fourth slide should detail the budget and personnel needed for the project, along with the projected timeline for completion.

Slide 5: Immediate Next Steps. Finally, your last slide further demonstrates your confidence and planning skills by detailing the immediate next steps to get the project up and running. This shows that you know where to start, and that you're ready to begin.

This simple approach to documenting your plans is a great way to influence most any audience. It's short enough to walk through in fifteen minutes, but packed with enough information that the leadership team can review facts and data and become comfortable with your recommendation. If you want to be known as an influencer across the company, be prepared to bolster your point of view with a crisp, data-driven presentation. Make it clean and professional looking (sometimes that's half the battle), and practice it with a peer or a team member before you deliver it. Influencing others is a vital skill to possess and be known for. If you want to break out and take charge of your leadership image, this is a great place to start. Develop your business case, present it with confidence, and start building your fan base inside the company!

Bootstrap
Takeaways

Give Great Presentations

1. Influencing others is an art. Do your homework to know how your boss likes to be influenced. What moves your boss to a decision?
2. Build a strong business case—most senior leaders respect and *expect* data. They want to see return on investment and a logical approach.
3. Keep your presentations concise—convey the information necessary to make a decision in just five pages.

38

A Healthy You

Bring Energy to Your Work

C'MON, YOU KNEW this was coming. A book about leadership development is not complete without this chapter; it must cover the "body" part of mind, body, and spirit, right? So far, we've explored various techniques and ideas for developing yourself as a leader—things to know, do, and believe that will help you lead with more confidence and style. But now we need to address your physical well-being. So here goes. I'm going to ask the awkward question: "How healthy are you?" There, it's out there. Now it's time to deal with it!

There's plenty of research that indicates people are more efficient and productive at work when they feel good physically. Seems obvious, right? For example, a landmark study, published in the January 2004 issue of the *Journal of Occupational and Environmental Medicine*, showed that workers who engage in moderate exercise have higher work quality and better job performance than those who lead sedentary lifestyles. According to the study, physically fit employees get along better with co-workers and take fewer sick days than out-of-shape employees. Subjects with high levels of cardiovascular fitness perform more work, using less effort.[16] That makes sense to me.

Would you say that your experience confirms this research? Don't you feel better at work when you're in shape, get enough rest, and eat right? Doesn't your confidence go up when you feel and look good physically? The fact is, in order to be a role model for professionalism, maturity, and values, you need to add one more facet to your leadership brand: Set an example for health and wellness.

Do What's Right for You

Each of us is at a different stage of life, which means we're each at a different stage of physical fitness, as well. I won't try to represent the avalanche of guidance that's available on dieting and exercise; you can seek out that advice on your own, and you've probably done so for years. Suffice it to say that you have to be honest with yourself about the relationship between fitness and work performance. Is your body enabling your mind and spirit to be at their best? If you're not comfortable with your stamina, focus, and concentration or your ability to maintain an even temperament, chances are your level of physical fitness is partly responsible.

Here's a story that reinforces the importance of paying attention to your physical well-being. A few years ago, an executive at our leadership program talked about his struggle to prioritize health and fitness. He said he'd always rank ordered the important things in his life as follows: family, work, faith, and health. Then, an event in his life triggered an epiphany about his own mortality, and he told the group he'd reordered his life priorities to be: health, family, faith, and work. He realized that he couldn't do his family or the company any good if he wasn't first taking care of *himself.* The irony was that this guy worked out regularly; he was in the gym every morning and had always enjoyed keeping himself fit. But it took a critical event for him to realize just how much his own health and well-being affected everything else in his life. When you're not healthy, that's not good for the family or the job. So here's the advice, as generic as it may sound: Get in the shape you need to be in to be optimally productive on the job. Don't let a lapse in physical fitness be the reason you don't succeed or get ahead in the organization.

A helpful insight comes from Jim Loehr and Tony Schwartz in their terrific 2003 book titled *The Power of Full Engagement*.[17] The authors believe that managing your energy (as opposed to managing your time) is the key to high performance. The premise is that as you age, you still have the same number of hours in the day but not the same energy levels. Maintaining your energy level is the key to sustained productivity and engagement. Again, this sounds reasonable to me. So, we have evidence that physical fitness is linked to performance, and common sense tells us that having more energy makes you more productive. Check. But now what? Ah, that's the question isn't it? You don't need to be convinced that being healthy makes you a more productive leader; you already knew that. And you also probably know what *you* should be doing about it, too. Still, something's holding you back. What is it?

The first step is to establish a baseline measure of your current state of health and wellness. Schedule a physical, either with your doctor or a company-sponsored clinic or hospital program. Find out from a medical professional what needs the most work. Then, actually follow the advice. You owe it to yourself to know the status of the machine you walk around in all day. Remember, you can't lead if you're not in the game. Second, a strong body of research is accumulating about sleep and its impact on performance. Turns out that going to sleep and waking up at the same time every night (i.e., a regular sleep pattern) is as important (if not more important) than the number of hours of sleep you get. Examine your own sleep rituals; how can you create a more consistent pattern to get the sleep you need? Third, assess your diet, or seek the advice of a dietitian. What and when you eat affects your energy and stamina at work.

Finally, pinpoint how your energy enables or hinders your performance by asking yourself three questions: 1) "What gets you excited about work?" 2) "In what part of the day do you have the most energy?" 3) "Who do you draw energy from?" To answer the first question, take all of your major work activities and cluster them into "buckets"; you might come up with a list that includes team meetings, spending time with direct reports, client visits, planning sessions, doing email, and so forth. Then, assign each a simple rating (use a 1-to-5 scale) in terms of your personal engagement. What do you enjoy most about your job? What do you enjoy least? The trick is to do more of what gets you excited and less of what doesn't. Remember delegation (Chapter 14)? Think of delegation as an alternative energy source; give away work with one eye on your own energy level. Also, you will find natural reserves of energy for the tasks you enjoy the most, so it makes sense to pair your best energy time frames with the tasks that drain your energy most often. That's the idea behind knowing what part of the day is best for you in terms of peak energy levels. If you're at your best in the morning, schedule your least favorite activities before lunch; you'll benefit by being alert and attentive for them. Likewise, interacting with people you really enjoy can carry you through the post-lunch hour; if that's typically a low-energy time for you, schedule one-on-one meetings with your favorite coworkers. Because certain colleagues may really energize you and others, conversely, may literally zap energy from you, it's important to identify who those people are, when you tend to deal with them during the day, and how you can make effective changes.

The simple fact is that work is tiring. It always has been, probably always will be. As a result, it helps to be healthy, well rested, and in shape. You owe it to yourself and your team to bring your best to work each day, and that's easier to do when you feel good physically. This might be your biggest leadership challenge yet:

How do you lead yourself down the path to better wellness? Whatever you decide, don't wait to get started. This is one development project you can't put off until next year.

Bootstrap
Takeaways

Bring Energy to Your Work

1. Your health and wellness dictate your energy and productivity. Know where you need to be in terms of physical well-being, and set a plan for getting there.
2. Consult health professionals for this development project. How can you best determine your current state of fitness and set and meet fitness goals?
3. This is something that no one can make you do—you must have the discipline and mindset to make the changes you want to see in yourself.

39

Write Your Own Screenplay

Imagine Yourself in Future Roles

ARE YOU ENJOYING the journey outside of your Comfort Zone? How's it feel to be trying some new things? You *are* trying to expand yourself, right? Are you pushing yourself out of your normal routine? Meeting some new people? Looking at things through a wider lens? Admitting that you don't have all the answers? Great, that's exactly what you should be doing. You won't grow and develop new skills if you don't challenge yourself differently than you have in the past. Think of it this way: If you always do what you've always done, you're always going to get the same results. You *have* to break out and take charge of your development in new and exciting ways, or you won't grow as a leader.

Here's an exercise that *really* challenges you to look at things differently: Visualize yourself in a different role, environment, and industry. That's right—take another step outside the Comfort Zone by imagining what you'd be doing if you weren't in your current organization, doing this particular job. Now you might ask: "What does this have to do with developing my leadership skills?" Good question, but let's withhold the answer for awhile and get into the exercise.

Start with Your Dream Job

What is it that you love doing? Don't think in terms of a specific role when answering this question; instead, write down the activities that get you excited. Do you like solving problems? Teaching people? Building relationships? Doing deals? Building a business from scratch? Developing a team? What is it that you enjoy most (the list might include things you haven't gotten a chance to try yet). What work-related activities motivate you most? Limit your list to five; you'll find that's enough to give you a clear view of your dream job. If you could build a job that allows you to do these five activities most of the time, wouldn't that be great?

Next, rank order the following work environments from most to least desirable: large corporation, small company, consulting or professional services firm, nonprofit organization, government agency or public service, independent contractor. There may be other career options, but these six cover most of the bases. What's right for you? Again, be honest with yourself. What appeals to you as you look ahead to the rest of your career? It may not be the current situation you find yourself in today. In my case, I've worked in all of these environments with the exception of government, and each of them has something different to offer. Early in my career, I worked in a small consulting firm, which required me to learn all of the parts of the business; we were so small that we all had to pitch in and do the little things. Later, I went to a small company, where I felt a real sense of purpose and inclusion; even though I was young, I got to be part of the management team that was striving to grow the company. Then I had the privilege of working in some well-respected large corporations, where I really felt the mission and excitement that comes with working for a winner. Later, I served on the board of a nonprofit organization and now work as an independent consultant, which gives me the flexibility and freedom to meet new people and broaden my skills. Clearly, the sum of those experiences has made me who I am today, just as your experiences have shaped you. As you look at this list, consider where your heart is leading you. Are you in the environment that's right for you, or are you ready to move to a different type of organizational structure and experience?

Finally, think about what industries or market segments interest you most. Are you fascinated with alternative energy? Are you drawn to life-saving industries such as health care or pharmaceuticals? Have you always wanted to work outdoors rather than in an office? What about public service? Do you like knowledge worker industries (technology) or customer interface businesses (travel, entertainment)? Give thought to the products and services that you really want to be associated with; from there, it's a quick leap to which specific companies you might want to work in. This exercise is pretty simple, isn't it? You've now established *what* you want to do, *where* you want to do it, and the type of organizational *environment* that seems best for you. Congratulations, you've just created your imaginary "dream role" scenario.

How Does This Help Me Today?

Now let's answer the question: "What does this have to do with developing my leadership skills?" Have you figured it out yet? There are three reasons to take a step back and imagine your dream role. First, it elicits the realization that this is *your* responsibility. If you don't first dream it, then chances are it won't become reality—no one else can envision the perfect job or career for you. Did you even realize these things about yourself? In my coaching practice, I repeatedly ask executives to do this exercise, and I'm continually amazed at how many have never thought about their skills or career in this way. You need to know these things about yourself: what you enjoy doing, where you would like to do work, and the type of organization you prefer. Give yourself the gift of reflection and insight—in this case, into your own hopes and dreams.

The second reason to do this is rather obvious: If this is what you want, how can you make it happen right now, in your current role? Think about your answer seriously. You already have the power to change how you spend your time, so make sure the majority of it is spent doing the things you enjoy best. As for what industry your firm is in, OK, so maybe you can't change that overnight. But maybe you can drive innovation that helps your company discover new products or markets, or maybe you can open new business channels with a little creativity. That might take you closer to the type of industry you want to be in. What about your environment? If you work in a large bureaucratic company but prefer a smaller environment, invent ways to make your corner of it feel like a small, entrepreneurial start-up. If you work in a small company but prefer a large corporate environment, create ways to add discipline and process to the way things get done, just like the big guys. How can you help your team be more consultative, or perform better in service to others?

Finally, this exercise may help you when the time comes to think about taking on a new career challenge (either inside or outside the company). You're bound to face this decision several times in your professional life. What are you using to guide those assessments? Knowing what you want to do, where you want to do it, and who you want to do it with helps to clarify the choices and point you in the right direction.

The point is this: It's great that you're busy in your current role; you're dedicated to your team and the company, and hopefully, you're happy there. But you need to write your own career story as you go along, and to do so you need to envision your career a few years down the road. After all, if you don't know where you want to go, no one else will, either. Identify what's important to you, and follow your heart. You just might take the first steps on a whole new leadership journey!

Bootstrap
Takeaways

Imagine Yourself in Future Roles

1. Think ahead to the next stretch of your career journey: What do you want to do? What interests you? Where do you want to do it and with whom?
2. Document your desired activities, industries, and work environments. Have a clue about where you might want to be at the next stage of your career.
3. This is something that only you can do—no one can do this for you. Take an interest in your own future, and be ready to take a potentially big step outside your Comfort Zone!

40

Question Everything

Review Your Strategy Twice a Year

AS A LEADER, how confident are you that you're doing everything right? How do you know if things are working as they should? How do you know when it's time to retire a particular product or process or to move into a new line of service? Let's say you have a sound overall strategy—every indication is that you're on the right path as far as your overall focus is concerned. But are you sure everything associated with that strategy is being executed well and, perhaps more important, still fits the strategy? Are you sure everything's on track? Some things you can measure, of course, so you should have a good idea of where you stand with the budget, your team's level of engagement, and customer service. But how are the components that make up the strategy, such as products, processes, services, marketing, pricing, and so forth, holding up?

One of the traps that inexperienced leaders fall into is assuming that if the overall strategy is sound, then the individual elements must be working just fine. That isn't always the case, especially if there are many moving parts involved. It's easy to get caught up in the "if the strategy is working, we must know what we're doing" syndrome. But here's where your continued development as a leader comes in: You have to learn that the right time to question everything is precisely when everything seems to be working. It's dangerous to think you've got everything figured out for that's usually when trouble sneaks up on you. At the same time, however, it's counterproductive to second-guess your every move. You have to trust that you and the team have built the right set of strategic drivers, and focus on execution. So, what's a smart leader to do?

Review the Elements of Your Strategy
Twice a Year

There is a way to balance healthy paranoia with the "full steam ahead" approach when it comes to evaluating the elements of your strategy (see Chapter 10). Twice a year, meet with your team and conduct a half-day strategy review session to ensure your action plan is on the right track. Schedule the meeting for the morning (when the team's energy level is high) and focus on the simple question: "How are we doing?" Establish a set of operating principles for the meeting so that everyone understands the ground rules. Among other things, agree to let all opinions be heard, remain objective in your assessments, and complete the meeting on time. Oh, and one more thing: This meeting works best when you step out of your Comfort Zone as the leader and participate as a regular member of the team. Yes, you might have to break a tie here and there, or weigh in if you have information that the others don't, but resist the urge to use a directive style here. Your objective is an honest evaluation of how the strategic components are working, and you won't get it if you're constantly interrupting or dominating the conversation. For at least two mornings a year, take a step back and listen to what your team members have to say; let them drive the dialog and write on the whiteboards (think of it as a development opportunity for you and a chance to assess the quality of their thinking, teamwork, etc.).

Once you've set the ground rules as a team, there's a simple tool and process that will help you find the answers. First, list everything you can think of in your portfolio, that is, everything your team is responsible for delivering. When I was leading Organization Development (OD) teams in my corporate life, we used to say that everything we did was a process, tool, program, or service; our entire list of deliverables would naturally fall into one of these four buckets. Whatever the main categories might be for you, try to fit your inventory into some type of structure; this will show whether you're under- or overweight in one element of your strategy. For example, the first time we listed everything we did, we noticed that we were woefully short on employee self-service tools, so that became something that we tried to drive with our new strategy.

Now that you have your version of programs, tools, processes, and services up on the board, evaluate each item in your portfolio using the Strategy Review Model found in Figure 7. Draw this four-box structure on the board, and write your mission and strategy statements above the grid to remind you of what you're trying to accomplish. Then, let the team fill in the boxes, moving each item from the inventory onto the grid. Try to keep quiet during this process (I told you this would require you to get out of your Comfort Zone!). Sit back, observe, and listen; let the team lead the discussion.

Obviously, the goal here is to see if everything still fits the strategy, and whether or not you need to improve execution. The easiest decision involves those items that don't fit your strategy and aren't being well executed (the Stop quadrant). Shut down those programs, processes, or services. They are wasting resources, customers probably aren't happy, and they're hindering your plan going forward. Assign someone the task of coming back to the team with a "stop" plan, and move on (don't solve this particular challenge in the meeting). For deliverables that are being well executed *and* fit the strategy (the Continue quadrant), congratulations—these are keepers; simply continue to maximize these items and reevaluate again in six months. The elements of your portfolio that still fit the strategy, but aren't being well executed (the Improve quadrant) are items that show promise, so it's worthwhile to try to make them more effective. Again, assign someone to be "on point" for coming up with an improvement plan that you can review at your next regular meeting. Finally, if you find that you're doing some things really well, but they don't fit your strategy anymore (the Export quadrant), it's time to figure out where in the organization you can move those deliverables (for example, we would routinely find things that we were doing in OD that were better suited for another HR group's mission and strategy). You may have to give up the resources used to execute this process or program, but if it doesn't fit your strategy, you need to do the right thing and move it into the right department. Take your time, and discuss each item thoroughly; the model helps you determine whether everything still fits and what you need to work on in terms of continuous improvement.

This simple format seems to work well as a biannual review process. As you "unpack the bag" and objectively evaluate your portfolio, it also gives you a chance to evaluate your team members. What are they excited about? How do they assess and discuss each item? Who's being objective vs. lobbying for a favorite area of accountability? How do they debate with one another? Are people interacting constructively? By putting your ego aside and allowing the team to lead what is a critical evaluation of your complete portfolio, you're developing the ability to see your team and its deliverables from an objective point of view. This is great practice for the larger leadership roles ahead, where you'll be expected to excel at this type of activity. If you've never conducted this type of meeting before, set one up and give it a go. It's a great way to hone your strategy, develop and assess the team, and work on your own leadership skills, all at the same time.

Bootstrap
Takeaways

Review Your Strategy Twice a Year

1. Step back and take an objective look at your deliverables: What are you doing well? How do they fit your strategy?
2. Let the team take the lead—this process is an effective way to develop your peoples' strategic thinking skills, and you can observe how they work together as a team.
3. Be prepared to stop or give up some elements of your portfolio when they no longer fit your current strategy.

Part Five

It's Not about You

IN MY CAREER, I've been fortunate to work with some wonderful CEOs, one of whom was Richard Fairbank at Capital One. Mr. Fairbank had a phrase that he used when talking with leaders throughout the company: "It's not about you, it's about them." What he meant, of course, is that leadership is about the people you lead—in the end, it's not about you. Which beg the questions: Is this how you look at leadership? Is this how you approach your role as a people manager? If not, what if you *did* see yourself as a servant leader? What would it change for you?

Perhaps this starts with how you prioritize your time as a leader. Do you spend your time on the right big things? Is one of those things people development? What if you were to go out of your way to raise the profile of your employees, sharing their accomplishments with the boss or positioning them with senior management? What if, in addition to your regular job, you were to volunteer your skills to mentor others who could really use the expertise, inside or outside the company? Do you make it a priority to offer others feedback and support? One of your obligations as a leader is to help others improve *their* skills. How about teaching a class at the corporate university? That's a great way to "give away" your knowledge and expertise. Are you up for that? How well do you listen? Are you where you want to be as a patient, attentive conversation partner? Finally, what is your plan for succession? How are you preparing the leader who will follow you? These are the questions that facilitate your transition from "it's about me" to "it's about them."

Be the leader who puts his or her people first and works hard to help them advance. Be the leader who always pitches in when things get tough and who puts the company's interests ahead of his or her own. Be the leader others admire for passion and self-lessness. If you want to truly make a difference as a leader, adopt the phrase "it's not about me" and see where it guides you. You'll be happy with the results.

(41)

It's All about Them

Showcase Your People

THE FUNNY THING about leadership is it's not about you at all. Isn't that something? All this hard work to develop yourself and it's not even really about you. It's about your direct reports and their teams, the people who benefit most from your improved leadership. Oh sure, you get something out of it too—the broader your skill set, the more attractive you are to your current (and future) employer. And leading more effortlessly gives you confidence, allows you to do more, and sets your career on an upward trajectory. But let's go back to your team and the whole essence of leadership, which is to help a group of people do more than they think they can do. In the end, leadership is about people; it's about developing and growing *their* knowledge, skills, and abilities. It's about helping them pull themselves up by *their* own bootstraps. This brings us to one of your obligations as a leader: showcasing your team to the organization.

If you're the only one who knows how great your team is, you're not doing all you can to advance your peoples' reputations in the company, which it turn, fuels their careers. You are their sponsor, their guardian angel, and there are two primary ways you can and should represent your people to the organization: 1) gain exposure and recognition for the entire team and their accomplishments, and 2) support specific team members (your best people) who are destined for greatness. In the former, you are charged with making sure the team gets the credit they deserve for big wins. There are a lot of ways to do this, of course, but the key is to pick your spots and be humble and gracious when you choose to toot your own team's horn. Various teams across the company do great work, and you'd do well to lead the cheers when it's time to recognize those groups. But don't forget to speak up on behalf of your team, too. Make sure your peers and especially your boss *and* your boss's boss know about the group's successes. Focus on results; no one wants to hear about how hard the team works—everyone works hard. Also, and I hope this is clear by now, when you praise the team, leave yourself out of the accolades. This isn't about you, remember? People will know the impact you had; after all, you put the team in a position to succeed with a great vision, mission, and strategy, and you coached them to the finish line. There's no need to make a big deal about it—that's what you are supposed to do as the leader. I've seen this done well, and I've seen it done poorly throughout my career, and I'm sure you have, too. Don't be like those bosses with the big egos who have to be in the spotlight and make it all about themselves. When you talk about your group and what they've achieved, make it all about the team.

Showcase Your Star Players

Let's return to the topic of your responsibility to sponsor your best talent. It feels great to watch the people you've developed succeed and advance their careers. And you have a significant role to play in this; in fact, it's nearly impossible for your people to be recognized and move forward without your support. If you say they're average or just OK, chances are the company will take your word for it. Likewise, if you choose to sponsor and endorse someone, the company likely will trust you and take notice. Here are three things you should do to showcase your star players.

First, ensure they get regular exposure to your boss. Take them with you to update meetings when they're the lead performers on particular projects, and gradually let them drive more and more of the discussion. Ask your boss to meet with them without you to get a sense of their talent and quality of ideas (a reverse skip-level meeting; see Chapter 44). The next time your boss delegates something to you that has visibility across the department or company, ask your boss to consider your star player instead. Then, ask your boss to coach or mentor that person throughout the assignment. Set up your boss and your employee with quarterly or biannual lunches, so they can get to know one another in an informal setting. In other words, get out of the middle and let your boss and your star performer develop a relationship. Bosses prefer to form their own opinions before they decide to join you in sponsoring an employee to advance in the organization—and it's your job to facilitate that process.

Second, your peers play an important role in how your boss sees your people. If your bosses are anything like the ones I've had, they're asking about your experience with your peers' team members. If they're doing this objectively, it's OK and understandable; they're just gathering as many data points as they can about the people on their teams. Just know that if the boss is asking you about their talent, he's definitely asking your peers about *your* people. Be prepared to leverage this experience. How? By putting your best players in a position to succeed with your peers. When you partner with a peer on a project and it goes poorly, take personal accountability for the issues. Talk up your best talent with your peers at every opportunity; make it very clear who your "go-to" people are. Before long, your peers will know who your star players are (this comes in handy at performance management time when you have cross-calibration meetings). Basically, repeat many of the boss techniques above: Arrange for quality time between your stars and your peers through projects, task forces, and presentations. Don't underestimate how important your peers' perspectives are on how the boss (or ultimately the organization) views your talent.

Third, your organization may have a formal way for you to represent your best players. The talent review or succession planning process is your opportunity to showcase your people, perhaps even in front of the senior team or CEO. Bring a lot of passion to the conversation, but be careful to present a balanced view of their abilities and potential; no one's perfect, and it will hurt rather than help when you're not objective or when you go overboard with praise. Stress the following three attributes that every senior leader wants to hear: your performers' strategic thinking skills, their work ethic, and their ability to collaborate and partner with others. These are the talent "holy grail": Can they think, do they work hard, and are they good team players? Nearly every employee contribution branches out from these three critical capabilities.

Finally, in all my years of leading teams, I always tried to pick out one or two people in each team to really push through the organization at an accelerated pace. I gave my best talent more of my time (frankly, I just enjoyed spending time with them) and found more challenging assignments for the star players. I loaded them up with the toughest and best opportunities, to sharpen their skills, yes, but also to test them. I showcased them to my boss and peers, took them with me on strategic meetings across the organization, and introduced them to other leaders around the company. I made it my mission to raise their profiles, oftentimes pretty quickly (hey, if you've got someone special, start stretching them early). Finally, what I really tried to do with my best talent was keep them in the company, even if it meant losing them to other teams. Using promotions, raises, and interesting and challenging assignments, I tried to "export" them to other departments and keep them moving up the career ladder. Sure, it's painful to give up top performers, but you owe it to them to not stand in their way when they're ready to make greater contributions.

The direct manifestation of "it's not about you, it's about them" begins with putting your best talent in the spotlight with your boss and your peers, and it continues through the performance management or talent review process. Pick out a star on your team and build a focused acceleration plan for that person; put the full weight of your reputation as a trusted talent evaluator behind his or her career, and watch it soar. Nothing will make you feel better as a leader than looking around the company some day and seeing several people that came up through your team. In the end, that's what leadership is all about.

Bootstrap
Takeaways

Showcase Your People

1. Put your people first by actively looking for ways to put them in positions to succeed. Stretch them with assignments that get them in front of your boss.
2. Spend the majority of your time with your star players. It sounds counterintuitive, but it's the right thing to do; develop your best talent.
3. Share your team's achievements, but do so with the right amount of humility and grace.

42

Give Something Back

Help a Nonprofit Organization

HOW DOES IT FEEL to take charge of your own leadership development? Is your hard work paying off? What differences have you
noticed? Better yet, what has your team noticed? How about your
boss or your peers? If you've done your homework, you should
feel good about the changes you've made; becoming a better leader
gives you more confidence, and frankly, it simply feels good to
be in touch with your advanced skills. Not only is it important to
you, it's great for your team and the company. When you improve,
the team becomes more productive and the company builds more
leadership capability. This is part of the implied employment contract: You work to improve your skills and the company benefits—
it's a case of a rising tide lifting all boats.

But you and the company both know that these new skills and
behaviors are completely transportable. Even as the company in-
vests time and money into your development, it knows that you
will likely apply those skills elsewhere someday. You know that
too, which is why you've taken charge of your own development.
You can't just sit around and wait for the company to develop you.

Another reason to develop your leadership skills has nothing
to do with your job or your career but has everything to do with
how you apply these new behaviors *off* the job, in other parts
of your life. Hopefully, you're using what you learn to fuel other

passions. Maybe your improved leadership is rubbing off on the kids you're coaching (those six-year-olds seem more engaged, right?). Maybe you're stepping up and leading more effectively on the school board or church committee or in other corners of your life. With any luck, working on your leadership skills is even making you a better parent, spouse, and friend. You can lead in all kinds of situations—anywhere people come together to set goals, solve problems, and accomplish something together.

Here's one more place to apply your new skills outside of the office: Put your leadership to work for a nonprofit group in your community. Whether you work for a large organization or a small company, you have skills that can be of great use to a local charity, foundation, or volunteer group. The experience of those who manage people, set strategy and lead change can be a real asset to these organizations. They need your help, and you could use the complementary leadership experience (it's likely to be very different than your current role). Here are three ways you can contribute while developing yourself as a leader in a nontraditional setting.

Leverage Your Functional Skills

First, offer a nonprofit your services as a consultant (pro-bono, of course) or mentor in your functional area of expertise. If you're an accountant, offer to review and assess the financial tools and procedures. If you're an IT professional, offer your expertise in evaluating the group's systems and making recommendations for upgrades, for example. Whether your field is marketing, operations, business development, HR, etc., look for ways to offer your functional or technical expertise to review current processes or design new ones. You can also serve as a coach or mentor to the incumbent or staff in your functional area. Determine knowledge or experience gaps and offer your advice and guidance (this is a great platform for practicing your mentoring skills). Whether you're "doing" or "teaching" from a technical perspective, set specific boundaries or parameters for the project. Be clear about where help is required, how you can assist, and how long the engagement will last.

Put Your Leadership Skills to Work

Second, put your leadership skills to the test and offer to lead a program or campaign. Nonprofit groups are eager for volunteers to help organize and lead funding campaigns, pledge drives, charity events, and other functions. This is another great way for you to practice your strategy, planning, and organizing skills. Sure, you can command a bunch of people who report to you at work, but can you influence and earn the trust of volunteers with whom you who don't have a formal reporting relationship? The challenges are different, and whereas you may use many of the same management techniques, this process will stretch you in ways you wouldn't be stretched on the job. How are you at juggling deadlines and multiple personalities? How are you at dealing with the public? What's it like to take on responsibility for something that is a little bit beyond your control? How about getting the job done with limited resources? OK, so you're familiar with that last one! The point is that lending your leadership talents to the challenges of a nonprofit campaign provides you with rich experiences unlike those you face back on the job. For starters, the stakes are usually high; fail to raise enough money and the organization's future may be at risk (do you have that much control over whether your company stays in business?). Also there's an emotional commitment that you naturally feel from being part of something so important. What can you learn from the engaged and passionate staff? What will you take away from this experience that you can apply back on the job?

Finally, you might be able to serve in an even larger capacity by taking a seat on the group's board of directors. Your strategy and leadership skills would be particularly useful at this level, especially if you have senior leadership team experience. Serving as a board member puts you in touch with a wide variety of executives and public officials that you probably wouldn't otherwise meet; builds your skills in shaping policy and strategy; and exposes you to budgeting, regulatory, and social challenges uncommon in your day job. It's a very rewarding experience that every leader should try at least once.

Decide to Make a Difference

At this point, I hope you're thinking: "You know, I've always wanted to do this. How do I get started?" Well, I'm glad you asked, because the very act of getting involved is development in its own right. First, get in touch with your own passions: What would get you excited about putting in extra time for a mission-driven cause? What organizations are doing work that gets you energized? Next, search online for local charities, nonprofits, or volunteer groups, and do your homework. There's bound to be several nonprofit groups in your area that can fulfill your enthusiasm for getting involved. Finally, contact them and go in for a visit. Ask to meet with the executive director, describe what you can contribute, and see what happens. Don't be shy about sharing your expertise and how you'd like to lend a hand. At the same time, be open to starting out as a volunteer; the group members may need to get to know you before they invite you into a consulting or leadership role.

When you connect with a nonprofit organization that matches your passion, not only do you build new skills and apply your leadership talents in a different venue, but you also gain experience and the reward of giving back to the community. And that might be the biggest gift of all—one that you give yourself.

Bootstrap
Takeaways

Help a Nonprofit Organization

1. When you decide to do this, jump in with both feet. This takes commitment and dedication, but the rewards are worth it.

2. Figure out what moves you: What are your passions? How can you best help your local charity or nonprofit?

3. Determine how you can make the greatest contribution, and volunteer your skills for a good cause—the experience will make you a better leader.

43

What the Boss Needs to Hear

Provide Feedback Up the Ladder

LET'S SAY YOU'RE SAILING along in your leadership role. Your team is knocking the ball out of the park, you're influencing major decisions across the organization, and you're about to launch a new product that will dramatically increase revenue. In short, things couldn't be better. Oh, and you're also happy with your development; you can feel yourself becoming more confident as you add new dimensions to your leadership toolkit. Everything's good, right? Well, except one little thing: your boss. Somehow your boss, who was an absolute rock of stability, has gone off the rails. Over the last several months, your boss has gone from being a trusted advisor to the CEO to teetering on the brink of irrelevance—which is *so* not good for you. What happened? And more important, what are you going to do about it?

There is no more important relationship at work than the one you have with your boss. Like two guide wires securing a footbridge, there are two main pillars of strength you need from your direct manager. The first is your boss's own reputation in the organization. When your boss is seen as ineffective, unreliable, or not living the values, that's a problem for your boss, of course, but also for you. If you've ever worked for a boss who was out of favor, you know exactly what I mean. Unless you're incredibly talented and insulated somehow (usually because you've found other sponsors), you're going to get a little paint on you from this broad brush. Your entire department starts to lose influence; you begin to get fewer resources; senior leaders start to question everything; and so on. The second guide wire, of course, is your manager's relationship with you. How well do you work together? Does your manager trust you, giving you the latitude to make a few mistakes? Does your boss back you up with senior management? Does he or she like your ideas, have faith in your judgment, and ask for your opinion before making a decision? To have a great relationship with your boss is ideal, especially as a leader. There's nothing better than knowing your boss has got your back, freeing you up to make things happen with your team. But now your boss is in trouble. What do you do?

The Gift of Feedback

The one thing you *must* do in this situation is give your boss feedback. You owe your manager that. You need to ask if you can help, describe what you're noticing, and provide some feedback and coaching. I understand this might not be the easiest thing to do; especially if you haven't established a pattern of upward feedback in the past. But when things reach critical mass, it's time for you to pitch in. It's not about you, remember? In this case, it's not about the team, either; rather, it's about the third significant link in your work chain. This is about returning the gift of feedback and coaching.

Start by asking about your manager's world in your next one-on-one meeting. Sometimes your boss will bring up these issues without prompting, but many times you have to get the conversation started. You can do this directly or indirectly. Direct questions are as simple as: "How are things between you and the senior team these days?" or "How's everything going with the CEO?" Indirectly, you can broach the subject with questions such as: "What's on your mind today?" or "What's keeping you up at night?" The point is to get your boss talking about the job, his or her boss, or the company. If your manager doesn't want to talk about it in this meeting, that's OK; you've established an interest in his or her well-being and can come back to these questions next time. Eventually your boss may begin to confide in you. If so, dust off your very best listening and coaching skills, because you're going to need them.

When your boss responds, chances are he or she will understate the situation (saving face will be important) or place the blame on factors outside of his or her control (a natural reaction). In that case, focus on your boss's emotions, feelings, and reactions. Literally, ask: "How do you feel about that?" This is a perfectly legitimate question that doesn't get asked often enough "up the chain" (bosses are people, too). At this point, you may get more than you bargained for, but once you go down this path, stick with it. You've just crossed over into being a confidant or sounding board, and your opportunity to provide feedback is right around the corner.

This is a great position to be in as a direct report. If you feel comfortable with this, invite your manager to blow off a little steam about his or her own pressures on the job. Your boss won't do this with just anyone, so if you reach this level of confidence, you'll be establishing a true partnership of trust. In my career, I always tried to establish this kind of relationship with my managers. I wanted them to know I cared about them, wanted them to do well, and was willing to listen if they wanted to talk about their own challenges. I would routinely ask about their standing in the company, with questions such as: "How are things going?" "What are you worried about?" "Who is supporting you?" "How are your relationships with your peers?" I genuinely wanted to help by offering suggestions and ideas or merely giving them an ear to bend for a few minutes. Generally, I had a view of the situation that they didn't have, and they often found it valuable to see things from another perspective. I can honestly say that *all* of my "best boss" relationships featured this exchange of "upward feedback," which was beneficial for both of us.

What Are You Noticing?

If your boss has opened up to you and placed the issue(s) on the table, it's time for you to wade in carefully with your own data and perceptions. This is where you share what you're noticing about your manager's attitude or behaviors. This is tricky, to be sure. Be straightforward, mature, and professional, and speak from your own experiences or observations. Don't say: "I've heard" or "someone told me"; hearsay is not productive or well grounded. You need to describe your own observations and provide first-hand feedback. You might offer: "I've noticed lately that you have been upset with Bill" (cite examples) or "I know you didn't feel fully prepared for that presentation last week" or "It seems to me that the Finance group is ignoring you on this issue—what do you think?" Communicate what you're noticing and feeling; if it's delivered objectively and supportively, your boss will be interested and want to hear more. Essentially, you're creating an opening to share meaningful feedback. If you hold this in (or worse, whisper about it with your peers), you're not helping the situation at all. Your responsibility as a leader is to step up and take the direct approach to help your manager get back on track.

By taking a genuine interest in your boss's well-being and offering your unfiltered but constructive feedback, you'll get the issues out on the table. Then, use your coaching skills to help your boss work through some solutions. Ask: "What options are you considering?" or "What do you think is the best way to approach Bill about this?" or "What's your next move?" The idea is to start brainstorming with her about ways to turn things around.

Obviously, if you have some thoughts or ideas on how to fix things, this is where you suggest them. But stay in coaching mode first; ask a lot of questions. Be a good listener and guide your boss to an honest assessment of the situation.

Giving feedback to the boss isn't your primary job, but occasionally it's a necessary part of being a leader. If you're lucky enough to work in an organization that genuinely values feedback, it's probably expected of you and welcomed by your boss. If it's not the norm in your company, look for those times when you can offer specific observations. Feedback is truly a gift, especially when someone is struggling; and when you assume an attitude of "it's not about me," you summon the confidence to step up and lend a helping hand. In a strange way, telling your boss what you really think might be the best thing you could ever do for that person. After all, leadership is all about helping others—and sometimes that even includes your boss!

Bootstrap
Takeaways

Provide Feedback Up the Ladder

1. Build a solid, trusting relationship or partnership with your boss.
2. When your boss obviously needs support, ask if you can help; then offer your firsthand observations and feedback. Don't make this about "what you're hearing" from others.
3. Practice your coaching skills—help your boss find solutions.

44

Extend Your Reach

Spend Time with Your Broader Team

SOMETIMES THE BEST WAY to sharpen your own leadership skills is to focus on others. Making a concerted effort to spend time with other people has a way of opening up new insights and opportunities for you; you learn things you didn't know, experience things from other points of view, and open up possibilities for innovation. This sort of follows the logic of: "If you never get out of your office, how can you tell what's really going on?" By the way, you *are* getting out of your office, right?

One of the best ways to "get out there" is to hold regular "skip level" meetings with members of your extended team. Your direct reports receive a lot of your attention, but what about *their* direct reports? How much time do you spend with them? And how much of that time is just one on one, without their boss in the picture? Spending time with your extended team members is a terrific way to let them experience your leadership; it provides them an opportunity to ask you unfiltered questions, share their ideas and projects, and learn how the organization works at your level. You get to learn, too—about the issues facing your employees, how they view the company, and so forth. In fact, you might be surprised just how *much* you can learn. Here are four ways to spend time with your extended team members, why it's important to the team, and how each enhances your own growth as a leader.

Gain a Unique Perspective

The first way to skip your direct reports is to hold one-on-one meetings with members of *their* teams. These are key players on your team, people who do a lot of the real work and make things happen. Schedule individual meetings or lunches with each team member at least twice a year. Gather their perspectives by asking the following four questions:

1. What's going well?
2. What could we be doing even better?
3. What can I do to make your job easier?
4. What are you doing for your own development, and how can I help?

The first two questions send a message that you're willing to listen and are designed to get these team members talking about the organization or department's strengths and opportunities from their perspective. These questions intentionally solicit their unique opinions and show that you are sincere about wanting to hear their specific work experiences. It's important to start with the positive question, and don't allow them to avoid an answer; it's just as important to role-model the "search for what's working" as it is to listen to constructive feedback about the organization. The second two questions demonstrate that you're interested in helping them be productive while they grow and develop. Really listen to what they have to say in response to each question, and take notes.

If you spend the time to get them comfortable with you (be aware that they may be a little intimidated), you'll probably get some new insights that otherwise might be filtered on the way up the chain of command. Alleviate the pressure by explaining exactly why you're conducting these meetings, which is to get to know them, learn from them, and answer any questions they might have. Make sure to follow up on any commitments you make, and touch base with your direct report (their manager) on any specifics that you discussed that they should be aware of or act on.

What do you get out of this experience? Several benefits, but primarily it's a chance to work on your mentoring or coaching skills. Practice asking questions and active listening (see Chapter 49), and take the opportunity to expand your knowledge of the business; there is an excellent chance they know things you don't about how the business *really* works. Especially when discussing their development plans, switch to coaching mode to draw out their plans and commitment to working on their game. How do they benefit from spending time with *you*? First, they literally get to know you better, which is important for their continued commitment to you and the larger team. Second, they get the chance to be heard by someone more senior than their boss, and that's huge for showcasing their thinking and ideas. Finally, they'll feel more connected to the organization after they get a sense of the way you experience the company. It's truly a win for both parties.

Make It All about Your People

The second way to spend time with your extended staff is to conduct "insight sessions" with several team members. These meetings are essentially focus groups with a specific purpose. Strive to lead one of these sessions each quarter; the meeting should last about ninety minutes (one hour will feel too rushed) and should have a single topic or question to explore. I used to do this with some of the larger teams I had the privilege of leading. In the spring, I would gather some of the team members together to get their input on our department's strategy for the year; in the fall,

I would do an exercise on what's working well and what could be improved as far as employee engagement was concerned. No matter the topic, try to focus on a few themes only, to allow the group to really go deep in terms of their feedback. Don't just ask, "How are things going?" Have an agenda, and make it a meaningful dialog. Your development here is all about listening and gathering insights. Part of the reason to conduct these sessions is to get to know these team members better, but the main purpose is to learn and gain an appreciation for the ways others experience the company, the strategy, and by extension, your leadership. The extended team members get to help shape a specific topic or question that's important to the company. Again, both parties walk away with new perspectives and a feeling that they contributed to something meaningful.

Third, you should conduct "all-hands" meetings with your full team throughout the year. Depending on the pace of change, you might have several of these sessions to keep the group informed, aligned, and focused. Schedule these for sixty to ninety minutes, and leave plenty of time for Q&A. Your goal here is to clarify the vision, mission, and strategy and be a visible presence in leading change. What do you get out of this? There are plenty of benefits. First, you create the opportunity to polish your public speaking skills and become more comfortable leading a large meeting. Second, you gain practice in the art of developing a compelling meeting agenda. Third, you're able to work on your leadership presence and the small details of showing up as a leader; it's hard to overemphasize the overt and subtle messages of confidence that you send through your words and body language in these settings. What the team members take away, of course, is a better sense of what's really going on in the company. Let them ask as many questions as possible to ensure that they're clear on the main points of your message.

Finally, on a regular basis, extend your leadership team meetings to include another layer of the team. I used to hold weekly staff meetings with my direct reports, but once a month we would expand the group to include five additional members from *their* teams, so we could give more people exposure to our decision-making process and solicit their opinions and ideas directly. Although it wasn't practical to add the entire next layer of management to these meetings, by rotating the invitation to five people each month, we were able to get every next-level manager to our staff meetings about twice a year. This is a great way to "demystify" what goes on in your team meetings, and it better aligns the entire department on purpose, process, and decisions.

While you're pulling yourself up by your own leadership bootstraps (getting in touch with the fact that "it's not about you"), spend more time with your extended team. Make this part of your regular routine and leadership style, and give away the gift of your time and attention. Don't isolate yourself from the people farther down in your organization chart; they want to spend time with you. It's important that they get to know you and personally experience your leadership. In terms of your own development, you'll build more relationships, get in touch with what's really going on, and gain valuable opportunities to influence and empower people across your entire department. What a great way to extend your leadership!

Bootstrap
Takeaways

Spend Time with Your Broader Team

1. "Get out there" and spend quality time with your extended team—"skip over" your direct reports and go directly to the next level.
2. Be proactive and planful about this strategy—make these meetings part of your regular calendar and make them a priority.
3. Put your leadership development plan to work; practice your listening, speaking, and coaching skills.

45

Your Most Precious Resource

Set Priorities for Your Time

HERE'S A SERIOUS QUESTION: Do you know how you spend your time as a leader? Many leaders that I work with can't answer this question accurately. They are unable to precisely account for their fifty or so work hours a week. Typical responses include: "I spend a lot of time in meetings" or "I'm fighting fires throughout the week" or "I don't know; I get interrupted a lot." Yes, but what meetings, and why? Where are the fires originating, and what can be done to reduce their frequency? Why are you interrupted so often? If you want to break out and move up as a leader, you need to face this question now, while you still have time to develop good work habits.

Do you realize that time is your most precious commodity? Let me repeat that. Your most prized resource is time—specifically, *your* time and the way you spend it. Here's the simple truth: To be effective as a leader, you need to spend your time efficiently. Think of the ultimate leader: the president of the United States. The president's entire day is carefully planned, down to the minute. If it weren't, it would be chaotic and unproductive and not half as much would be accomplished. Effective time management is essential to your performance as a leader. You need to know where the hours (and minutes!) are going and feel confident they're being put to productive use.

Prioritize Your Focus Areas

Ironically, the first thing you have to realize is that you can't control time. The fact is, there are only twenty-four hours in a day, and that isn't going to change anytime soon. So it's not *time* you need to manage, it's *yourself*, and how you spend the time you have. Start by getting a handle on where your time goes. This means you need to track it. The study and teaching of "time management" is not new; it's a big business and there's no shortage of articles and seminars that preach the use of day-timers, to-do lists, and goal setting procedures. Tools can help, but it all starts with setting priorities.

Here's a simple process to get started. In your journal, write down your top three priorities. These are the three areas that you feel are highest in importance for you, right now. Because priorities change, you'll need to do this exercise often. Think in terms of a week or a month; those are the right blocks of time for this exercise. This week or this month, one of those priorities might be completing performance evaluations on your direct reports. Maybe the budget needs to be finalized, or maybe your priorities include the product roll-out, the sales trip, the board meeting, the restructuring communications, or the merger. You get the idea: Priorities are big things that demand your full attention.

As the leader, you have a lot of plates spinning, and it's easy to get distracted. So don't identify more than three priorities—part of this exercise is to get you to focus. The only way to be sure you're working on the right big things is to identify your biggest, most important areas of impact. Now, make note of how you're spending each hour of the day, in order to track how much time goes toward those three major priorities. For two full weeks, write down how you spend each hour of your day, and see how well you have aligned your time and your priorities. This is the hardest but most critical part of the exercise. It only takes a few minutes each day, but for some reason many leaders simply don't have the discipline to maintain the tally for two full weeks—those are the same leaders that fail to improve their time management. If this is important to you, stay with it; the first step to using time more wisely is to understand where it's being wasted.

Two weeks later you should have a clear idea of where you spend your time. If you've spent more than 75 percent of your time on your big three priorities, good for you; you're spending your time on the major issues. In any one week or month, you should spend three-quarters of your time on your primary tasks or initiatives.

However, like many leaders, if you didn't approach this level of productivity, your assessment is telling you that you're wasting your most precious resource. Now the question becomes, what do you do about it? How can you eliminate time wasters and maximize time spent on your priorities? There are no easy answers, but following are three useful strategies.

First, you need to delegate more effectively (see Chapter 14). Look closely at your notes; what did you do over the last two weeks that someone else could have done just as effectively? Give it away, and spend time doing that which only you can do.

Second, you probably need to say "no" more often. Decline that meeting that you don't really need to attend. Push back when your boss requests that ten-page report; ask instead to prepare a one-page summary. Guard your time as if it's your most precious resource, because it is. Distinguish between what's important and what's merely urgent. Many leaders erroneously spend too much time on urgent issues rather than their most important priorities. Resist the urge to fight fires, and stay focused on your three biggest priorities.

Finally, you might need more discipline at the margins of your day (first hour, last hour). Are you capitalizing on this time? These potentially productive hours may be wasted because of your personal habits of starting or winding down a day. Take a hard look at these hours in particular, and make the necessary changes to use them more efficiently. For example, if one of your priorities is employee engagement, rather than spend the first hour in your office reading the newspaper with your morning coffee, use that time to go out and talk to employees.

This brings me to the secret of prioritizing and spending your time wisely: You need to *declare* your intentions to yourself, to your team, and most important, to your boss. Again, you're in control here (or need to be). If you're not willing to identify and share your biggest priority items for the week or month, why should you be taken seriously as a leader? If you're hopping around from crisis to crisis, or wasting time in meetings you don't need to attend, you're a weak role model for discipline, focus, and clarity. Know what you need to *do*, and know where you need to *be* as a leader. Figure it out (set priorities) and do it (execute). You'll feel organized, energized, and productive. Be warned, though: People will definitely notice the change in you. That means you might need to spend some of your time teaching others to be more efficient!

Bootstrap
Takeaways

Set Priorities for Your Time

1. Set three priorities for the upcoming week or month, and then spend 75 percent of your time working on those critical focus areas.

2. Start by tracking the way you spend your time today. Make adjustments using delegation or by just saying no to nonessential requests.

3. Get disciplined about your priorities. If you're not spending time on them, who is? And what else are you doing?

46

Step Up to the Podium

Teach a Course Inside Your Company

IT'S OBVIOUS THAT PART of what you bring to your leadership role is a deep well of knowledge and experience. You've cultivated a deep understanding of your chosen profession, and you've experienced a lot in your career. It all adds up to a tremendous store of information and wisdom, and because you're a dedicated professional, you probably share those insights with others. If you coach your direct reports or mentor other colleagues, you're giving away that knowledge and expertise one person at a time. That's great; coaching and mentoring are reminiscent of the apprentice model in which a single student studies with a trusted master. But there's a larger role for you to play when it comes to sharing your experiences. You need to become a "leader as teacher" within your organization.

If you work in a large organization, this may be a lot easier than you think. Most large corporate universities welcome leaders who want to join the "faculty" and teach a few courses. Just contact your learning and development consultant and ask to get involved. They'll help you create content, give you feedback about your teaching style, and help schedule the classes. They'll even do the marketing for you, so people know when and where to find you on the training curriculum. Once you join the teaching staff, you'll probably meet other leaders who have already blazed a trail to the podium.

However, not everyone works in a big company and has these kinds of resources. If your company doesn't have a formal learning center, this process just takes a little bit more perseverance and ingenuity. Once your program is designed, look for various opportunities to teach the class, either by pitching it as a special event for individual departments or by offering your program to leaders who organize off-site meetings. Regardless of whether you have the infrastructure or support, here's how to become a "leader as teacher" in your organization and start delivering those valuable lessons to larger groups of people.

Develop Your Teachable Point of View

Outlined below are five basic questions to answer when you create your teaching platform.

1. **What are you good at?** The answer to this involves figuring out what you know that others could benefit from; in other words, in what areas are you a subject matter expert? If you're not an electrical engineer, you probably shouldn't teach that subject to the engineers in your company. Likewise, if you're a poor communicator, don't try to tackle the subject of effective communications. Maintain your credibility by identifying a subject that you're passionate about, know deeply, and actually have a reputation for being good at (otherwise, you'll be teaching to an empty room, won't you?).

2. **What is your teachable point of view?** Develop what Noel Tichy calls a "teachable point of view."[18] This means you need to find your voice: What do you want to say about this topic, and how will you say it? Will you share certain models or frameworks? Will you be espousing one particular theory over

another? Do you hold opinions or viewpoints that are controversial? In other words, what are you interested in sharing with others? Your teachable point of view probably needs to be vetted inside the organization. If your company is trying to reinforce a certain process and you believe it ought to be doing just the opposite, that's an obvious misalignment that probably won't be received well. This is the most important step in the process, so spend the time to ensure that your teachable point of view is meaningful, relevant, and aligned.

3. **How are you going to share your knowledge?** You must create a learning outline for the material. How are you going to share your expertise? Is it best delivered in a lecture format or through a lot of small-group work? Does it require experiential learning or passive learning, where the participants sit in a classroom and learn concepts through lectures? Do you request that the participants complete any preliminary work or reading? Develop a crisp delivery style, and by all means, make the course interactive—no matter how charismatic you are, no one wants to hear you lecture for two hours straight. A good rule of thumb is to follow this sequence of content, practice, and application: 1) present the theory, research, or best practices (content), 2) create exercises so that people may apply what they've just learned (practice), and 3) close by discussing practical ways to best use these skills back on the job (application). Include in the learning outline the length of the course or program: Is this a two-, four-, or eight-hour gig? Is it a single course, or do you have enough content to merit a multi-module approach? Figure out how best to share your teachable point of view, the optimal time for the course, and how it all makes for a compelling learning experience for the participants. Don't be shy about getting some help with this step from a teaching professional; there is an art to teaching, and you should strive for optimal impact.

4. **Who's the target audience?** Who should attend your class? Who will benefit from this information? That you have some expertise to share is all well and good. But does anyone really want (or need) to hear it? Is this must-have knowledge or skills content that is critical to operations, or is it information that's simply "nice to have"? Along with the question of who should sit in the classroom, determine the optimum number to share this experience with at any one time. Is it better to keep the group small (ten to twenty-five people) or does your message translate well to large groups (fifty to seventy-five people) who can easily absorb and use the content?

5. **What's your commitment?** Give some thought to your long-term commitment to teaching the course. If it makes sense to run two hundred managers through the program (twenty at a time), then you're signing up for ten events. Do you have the stamina for that? In my career, I have had the privilege of starting and running several corporate universities, and I've seen leaders begin with the best intentions but quit after delivering the course only once or twice. They simply gave up and backed out of their commitment when they got too busy or grew bored with the process. Needless to say, such actions neither benefit your reputation nor satisfy the needs of the people you had intended to take through the course. Decide ahead of time how often you want to teach the program, and then adhere to your commitment.

Teaching a course is one of the most rewarding things you'll ever do as a leader, and it truly represents a "give back" to the organization in terms of sharing your time, knowledge, and experience. Whether you take advantage of a large training infrastructure or chart new territory as a leader as teacher, you should enjoy this role. I always feel I've done something meaningful when I share my experiences with an audience. I feel like I've made a larger contribution that day—that I've helped a few light bulbs go on around the room about how to improve as a leader. I think you'll have the same experience. For starters, it sharpens your own knowledge and skills, because to teach something, you really have to know the content. But it's much more than that. This really isn't about you; it's about your audience. Just think of the number of people you can impact in this role. Find something you're passionate about and have a flair for teaching. Then step to the front of the room, grab the chalk, and make a difference.

Bootstrap
Takeaways

Teach a Course Inside Your Company

1. Figure out what you're good at—what can you teach with undeniable credibility?
2. Design the course with the participants in mind—what kind of experience is the most beneficial and enjoyable?
3. Make a commitment. Before you even design the course, be honest with yourself about your ability and willingness to sustain the process.

47

Talk to Yourself

Ask Three Questions Every Day

BY NOW YOU'VE FIGURED out that leadership is not about you. That's the basic premise, because when you add it all up, leadership is about others—period. You don't lead computers, desks, office buildings, contracts, raw materials, or other inanimate objects. The only thing you truly lead is other people. The leaders who understand this are the ones everyone wants to work for; these are the managers who annually get the highest engagement scores, have the lowest turnover, and get the best results. That's because they "get it." They know that leadership is not about them; it's about others.

You are striving to be such a leader. That's why you're pulling yourself up by your own bootstraps and putting in all this extra work. That's why you're willing to add new skills or try new techniques: because you "get it," too. You realize that you can *always* improve your leadership, that you're never too established to try something new or different to achieve even greater results.

Ask Yourself Three Questions

Here's another simple technique to remind yourself that leadership is not about you. Every day, have a conversation with yourself about your leadership impact. That's right; every day, talk to yourself about your progression as a leader. Later, when you get really good at this, you won't have to do it so often, but initially I recommend you follow this routine on a daily basis.

Now, I don't necessarily advise you to talk to yourself out loud. That might get you in all kinds of trouble, especially if you *answer* yourself (but if you must have a verbal conversation with yourself, by all means, don't let HR hear you). So make this a silent conversation, one that you have in your own head. Here's what I recommend: Every evening, on your commute home, ask yourself three questions:

1. "How did I show up as a leader today?"
2. "What did I communicate today?"
3. "Who did I develop today?"

The first question is broad in scope, so let's explore it. Every day, whether you work in a large company or a small firm, whether you see your team all day or manage remotely, you can and should do something for your team. Let me repeat that: *Every single day* you should show up as the leader and do something for your team. One of the most obvious things you do for your team members is to procure resources or approvals for their work. Another is to break down barriers or remove obstacles; a good leader always clears the way for the team to get stuff done. You may introduce them to the right people in other parts of the organization, recommend certain vendors, or point them to information or data they need to complete their tasks. Maybe you challenge them to innovate, reach for higher levels of quality, or incorporate best practices. You might introduce them to senior executives, write them a note of encouragement or thanks, keep them focused on their own work-life balance, or just be available to answer their questions. The point is, every day you act in service to your team. That's what you're there for, right? To serve the team? So, how did you show up as a leader today? Generate the list in your head or jot them down in your journal before you leave the office or when you get home. Either way, you should be able to quickly think of a few things you did for the team today that made their jobs easier and more productive.

Second, because communicating is such an important part of leadership, ask yourself: "What did I communicate today?" Frankly, if you're like a lot of leaders, there's a good chance you tend to *under*-communicate. Yet every day you have an opportunity to communicate with your team, even if it's just to touch base on a personal level. Beyond the normal interactions, did you provide any new information today? Did you share something about what's going on around the company to increases their sense of ownership or engagement? Did you translate strategy, explain a recent organizational move, or pass along communications from senior management? How did you connect them to the company's mission today? How did you inform, educate, or explain? This might not be an everyday occurrence, by the way. Some days there just isn't a lot of "new news." But keeping track of what, how, and why you communicate, gives you a real sense of whether you communicate often enough and whether it is has the desired effect.

I remember when I tried this process a few years ago with my team members. They were all in different locations, so I didn't see them face-to-face every day. I kept a daily log of what I communicated, and I was shocked to discover that I went for days without sharing *anything*. Turns out, by becoming disciplined about answering a simple question—"what did I communicate today?"—I revealed a startling behavior. Now, you might think: "They're big boys and girls; because you pointed them in the right direction, you didn't need to talk to them every day." Maybe so, but when I did step up my communications efforts, they greatly appreciated the increased flow of information. Trust me; it's hard to *over* communicate to your teams.

Finally, ask yourself: "Who did I develop today?" In many ways, developing talent is your number one job, and it's something you should do all the time. Who did you coach or mentor today? Did you provide anyone with an opportunity to present to senior management? Did you give someone a new task or a stretch assignment? Did you send anyone a book or an article to read? Did you meet with anyone to review a project and stimulate new ideas? Did you challenge anyone's point of view and make that person better for it? The point is that when you think about development as something you can do every day, chances are you will follow through daily. That's what this exercise is all about; when you put your mind to it, you can shift your thinking around to what's possible.

Try to ask yourself these three questions at the end of every workday for a month. Notice the patterns or trends that emerge and where you have opportunity for improvement. Do you practice servant leadership? Do you communicate useful information on a regular basis? Do you consistently develop your team members? Use the data as a baseline to track your progress and assess your behaviors, and step up your efforts to lead more effectively. Leadership is all about the team, so make sure *your* team gets your best every day.

Bootstrap
Takeaways

Ask Three Questions Every Day

1. Leadership is all about the team—it's not about you, it's about them.
2. Track your own behavior—every day, do you make things happen for your team, communicate information, develop your people?
3. Assess your daily habits—how does the team experience your leadership? Do you completely focus on helping the team excel?

48

Join the Volunteer Army

Donate Your Leadership Skills

THE FAMILIAR PHRASE "it takes a village" may be a bit overused, but its underlying message has relevance for your overall leadership contribution. OK, so you may not literally work in a village, but the organization you belong to certainly can be described as a community. After all, you do "live" with the same people, in the same environment and culture, to pursue a common purpose, yes? That's basically what work is: a shared community of people who are aligned around a common objective. This notion of community is rather significant and becomes acutely obvious when you change jobs. What's the most challenging thing about moving to a new organization? It's not the new role and its associated tasks; typically, you know how to perform your basic duties. It's the new culture you have to learn, the new people and unique norms; in short, your biggest hurdle is to learn your way around the new "village."

This feeling of community is quite real in many organizations. If you've ever worked at a company that you truly cared about, then you've experienced the feeling of belonging to something bigger than just another place to work. Hopefully, the concept of community captures your curiosity, and as a leader, sparks some questions for you, such as: "How can I contribute to the community?"

and "how can I leverage my leadership skills for the good of the company?"

Here's the deal: As you move up in the organization, your leadership needs to extend beyond your own team. That's right; you need to lead more broadly across the *entire* organization and not just your specific part of it. This is about you breaking out and taking a larger leadership role, beyond the borders of your department. As you rise up the ranks, you're expected to help define and shape the culture of the organization. This is about becoming a *community* leader, not just the head of your "household." You get the picture; as it becomes "less about you and more about them," you need to start leading a broader spectrum of people. In other words, you need to give more of yourself (and your leadership skills) to the cause.

Find Ways to Get Involved

Try this exercise: Jot down on a piece of paper the full extent of your leadership contribution over the last twelve months. Did you demonstrate leadership beyond your group or department? How did you contribute beyond your regular role? In my experience, the average manager or leader extends his or her leadership to fewer than three programs, projects, or events in any one year period. There are varied reasons for this, of course: You may be swamped with work this year, you may think you're too low in the organization to play a cross-functional role, or perhaps your department is out of favor at the moment and hasn't been asked to get involved. But take a look at the opportunities listed below. Could you see yourself adding value in these situations? What could you gain from applying your leadership skills more broadly across the organization?

1. Lead a cross-functional task force.
2. Serve as the chairman of a volunteer committee.
3. Be a board member for your corporate university.
4. Lead an advisory council for another department.
5. Manage a large-scale company event.
6. Take the leadership role for a special project.
7. Serve on a steering committee (e.g., benefits, reorganization, infrastructure, etc.).

There are many ways to put your leadership expertise to use inside the company, and all of them benefit you and the organization. Your company is filled with task forces, committees, councils, and special projects that are crying out for leadership. You'd be surprised how many opportunities there are to help manage and govern the company; you simply have to open your eyes to what lurks below the surface. And then, you have to be willing to play a larger role and "put yourself out there" as a viable candidate to lead. Organizations don't run themselves; there is generally an infrastructure of processes and policies that cross-functional working groups constantly evolve—and you can help shape these if you get involved. And because you're a leader, strive to be more than just a member of these groups. Stretch your skills by volunteering to *lead* one of these efforts. The additional experience you'll gain will net you new relationships, exposure to senior leaders, and an appreciation for how things really work inside the company. Yes, it means extra work for you, but in all likelihood, you'll get back more than you put in.

Start by looking around for something that interests you that already has an existing volunteer leadership role. Then meet with your manager and the sponsor of the project or group and ask to get involved. Choose working groups or opportunities that will stretch your current leadership skills. Step outside your Comfort Zone; if you're used to a command and control environment, the committee experience would be a nice change of pace (generally you can't dictate what gets done, so you'll have to develop your influencing skills). You may have to serve a year as a committee member before you can lobby to move up into a leadership role, but that's OK—that's a learning experience, too. Ask your HR representative to help identify a special project or event that currently lacks leadership, and volunteer to get it up and running.

Finally, think about *starting* a committee, task force or working group on a topic you feel the company needs to address. Ask yourself: "What's the biggest challenge facing our organization today?" This can be the most rewarding leadership challenge of all; contributing on this level is deeply gratifying. Does your company have a coordinated effort around volunteerism? How about looking systematically at cost control or integration opportunities? Has your organization started a sustainability project? Here is your chance to build something big from scratch! Not a bad way to make a difference, right?

Take the concept of "it's not about you" to a higher level— volunteer to serve in a leadership capacity that's outside your normal role. Give back to the company that's given so much to you by lending your leadership skills to a good cause or an issue that needs fresh thinking. Be that leader who's intimately involved in the fabric of the company, the one everyone points to as a model of true servant leadership. Find a way to contribute your leadership to the cause; you'll find it feels good to serve your community.

Bootstrap
Takeaways

Donate Your Leadership Skills

1. You have a lot to offer—spread your leadership expertise around the company by volunteering to lead a working group, task force, or committee.

2. Find something that stretches and challenges you; this is a great way to work on your "influencing without authority" skills.

3. Be known as a leader who pitches in and helps set the cultural norms in your organization.

---

(49)

The Best Advice Ever

Become a Better Listener

NOW THAT YOU'VE READ this far, you should have a few ideas for developing your leadership skills and taking your game to the next level. That's great. But let's say you're in a staff meeting or a one-on-one with a direct report and something is still nagging at you. You've gotten good at self-evaluation, so you know there is one critical skill left to work on. That skill is listening. You just aren't listening very well to the conversations around you. Oh, you hear the words, but you know you're not listening effectively. You know what? You're probably right. Many leaders aren't great listeners, and yet listening is one of the most important skills to possess as a leader. If you do nothing else to develop yourself, work on becoming a better listener.

When you consider that listening goes back as far as human speech itself, it's amazing that we're not better at it by now. How hard can it be? Someone talks; you listen. You talk; someone listens. It's so simple—and that's precisely the problem. Listening is so natural that most leaders don't see the need to get better at it; it simply doesn't bubble up to the top of the skills development list. In fact, if you were to ask one hundred leaders if they were "above average" listeners, about 95 percent would say yes. To illustrate the point, a few years ago a study revealed that people believed the voice messages they left others were more important than the ones they received. In general, we tend to believe *our* message is more helpful and urgent than the ones we receive from others.

Absorb What's Really Being Said

You are probably familiar with all the regular techniques for active listening: Lean forward in your chair, maintain eye contact, nod your head, paraphrase what you hear, ask questions, pause before you react, and so on. Continue to use these behaviors; they work and go a long way toward building your skills as a good listener. But the real issue isn't whether you merely demonstrate the behaviors of active listening. That you *reflect, absorb,* and *act* on what you hear is what establishes your reputation as a great listener.

When employees communicate with you, they do so with a specific purpose in mind. They either: 1) want something from you, 2) want to pass along knowledge or facts, or 3) want to articulate their feelings or ideas. When they decide how to express themselves, employees select the method that they believe most effectively delivers the message (whether verbal or nonverbal). Your job is to interpret the message for meaning and purpose. Here's the critical link: Effective listening happens when you receive and interpret the message in the same way that the employee intends it. So how do you maximize the odds of that happening?

First, do some *pre-reflection* about the person who sends the message. In order to listen effectively, you must develop a genuine interest in or respect for the other person. There has to be something that the employee thinks, feels, or wants that you believe is worth listening to; in other words, you must ground your listening in a legitimate *reason* for listening. It's common for us to tune out people we don't like or don't feel are important. I remember a senior executive that I worked with who didn't listen to me in meetings specifically because he didn't think he *needed* to listen to me; he had a preset attitude that there was nothing I could possibly say that he needed to incorporate into his thinking. I could have told him all kinds of outrageous stuff, and I doubt he would have even reacted; he literally didn't listen because in his mindset he had nothing to gain.

Try this: Before you sit down for a one-on-one meeting or walk into the weekly staff meeting, remind yourself why you need to listen to *each* person. What is the context? Where are they coming from? What's been valuable about their messages in the past? If you can't think of a single reason to listen, open your mind to the possibility that there just may be something new you can learn (and then listen from that perspective). Listening effectively starts with getting yourself ready to listen. Beforehand, consider the message they're likely to send, their usual style, your typical reaction to that style, and so forth. Get your head right first; by reflecting on past behaviors and *preparing* yourself to listen more effectively, you inevitably will.

Second, because people vary greatly in their communication style, you need to understand how your team members express themselves; you need to do your homework about how they articulate their needs and wants and their usual purpose for interacting. When meeting with an employee, what's typically most important to that person? People tend to communicate three basic types of information: facts, opinions, and feelings. Obviously, all three may be expressed in the course of one sentence—your challenge is to *absorb* the message and tease out what's most important. This is critical. Failure to recognize what's most important results in ineffective listening. You may have heard the words, but you missed the meaning they wanted to convey. This produces the classic "crossed wires" feeling that employees walk away with sometimes and leads to the "he didn't hear me" comments. You can ensure more messages hit their mark by reminding yourself of the three types of information above and paying close attention to what it is your employees are really trying to communicate. For example, when an employee tells you that he or she is upset about an interaction with a co-worker, it is important that you focus beyond the facts and acknowledge that person's feelings. Identify the purpose early, and then absorb the most important part of the message.

Once you have absorbed the most important piece of information, you need to *act* on it. Part of effective listening is responding appropriately; this tells the employee you heard them correctly. Articulating what you feel is the most important part of their message takes the conversation to the heart of what matters and leads more quickly to agreements or resolutions. Again, try this: When someone relays an opinion and it seems packed with emotion, ask about the emotional part. By paying close attention to what's most important, you can proactively take the conversation where it needs to go. As a leader, it's important not to be too passive or use active listening as a crutch; once you feel you've identified the most important part of the message, focus on it. Put it out in the open and deal with it directly. Put the "active" in active listening by moving on to solutions or a deeper conversation. For example, when an employee is angry with a co-worker, establish the facts, but also deal with his or her emotions; help the person see how negative emotions can impede a positive course of action.

Intuitively, you know there is a big difference between hearing the words and really listening to the message. It's not like you don't *know* that you need to listen and pay attention; the issue is that you don't always do it. And you know what? Improving your listening skills is a difficult task that takes a concentrated effort; you have to consistently work at it. Do this: Practice getting ready to listen by *reflecting* ahead of time on the person and his or her communication style. Next, practice *absorbing* what's most important from the person's message. Choose one of the three types, and label it in your mind. Then, *act* on what you're hearing, applying your leadership instincts to make something good happen as a result of the conversation. Becoming a better listener is one of the most effective ways to improve your leadership brand. Now that's advice worth listening to!

Bootstrap
Takeaways

Become a Better Listener

1. Get your head right—approach every personal encounter with an open mind and a feeling that you're there to listen and learn.
2. Find the true purpose of the message. Identify the most important piece of information and "hear" the conversation from that perspective.
3. Use what you hear to solve the right issues. Focus on the underlying message, not just the words, and then take the conversation in that direction.

50

Welcome the New Guard

Write a Letter to Your Successor

ONE OF THE MOST EXCITING things any leader can do is to take on a new role, be it in your current organization or in a new company. It's invigorating to apply your leadership skills in a new situation, develop relationships with new people, and craft a fresh strategy for a different set of challenges. Talk about development! Every manager should have the chance to move through a series of new challenges; in fact, that's what a career is all about—tackling a collection of different experiences.

When your chance comes to move on, there are a couple of things you should do before you leave your current role. One of them is to say thank you to everyone who has helped to make you successful. Do this in two ways: First, take the time to personally reach out to those who made a difference in your work life. Then, follow up with a handwritten note (a lost art these days) on attractive, professional stationary. The handwritten note is a classy gesture and reflects well on your leadership brand. The other thing you need to do, of course, is to prepare your successor. Be sure to brief this person on the team's strengths and opportunities as well as the key performance goals and challenges facing your group.

Hopefully, this is not a last-minute process because you've groomed your own successor. However, many times, a clear successor is not available—and even if there is one, sometimes you only have a day or two before starting the new assignment. In that case, there is a time-honored technique you can use to transfer critical information to the next leader.

Write a Letter to Your Successor

Writing a letter to your successor is a tradition that has its historical roots in military and political change-of-command scenarios. The idea is to leave a document that outlines your assessment of the situation and maybe even offers a few suggestions for immediate next steps. That way, the new leader doesn't walk in completely cold to the situation without a sense of the team dynamics, recent production developments, and so forth. Whenever you leave a leadership position, use this technique to leave your successor something to absorb about your team's current state of affairs. However, because this is about your development *right now*, we're going to borrow the "letter to your successor" concept as a way to sharpen your leadership today. In other words, if you implement this technique as a developmental exercise, you can use it to guide your *own* leadership agenda over the next several months. Here's how it works.

What Would You Do if You Were Staying?

First of all, take this process seriously, and treat it as if it were a real situation. Pretend that you're moving to a new role, and that you only have a day to transition your successor. You don't feel you have enough time to give away all your thoughts and ideas after a long day, so you've decided to write a letter to capture your final recommendations. Start the letter to your imaginary successor by listing in bullet format your impressions of the team's strengths and opportunities. Keep the lists brief; limit them to five to eight key strengths and three to four relevant opportunities.

Following this summary of the team's strengths and opportunities, write a top-ten list of the things you would recommend be done in the next ninety days. Title the list: "Ten Things I Would Do if I Were Staying in the Role." Note, this is not a new leader assimilation list; you're not giving the traditional "get out and meet your team members" type of advice. This list is just what it sounds like: a list of the actions you would take next if you were staying in the job. When I left AOL, I remember writing this exact letter to my successor, Linda Simon, and it felt really good to express in writing what I wanted to see happen to the group I was leaving. I was bold, too—I included ideas in that letter that even *I* hadn't tried yet, hoping Linda would find a way to implement them. It was quite liberating, actually, to have a say in how the team would move forward after I was gone. I think Linda appreciated the letter; I know for certain that she led the team to new heights over the next few years.

Your top-ten list should include the items that need to be tackled in the next three months. Make these items actionable; while it's OK to be provocative, make sure the ideas or suggestions can actually be implemented. Flesh out these ideas and be bold—this is your chance to write a new blueprint for yourself, a new leadership agenda.

Although this is a "pretend exercise," you can use it to make real, positive change happen; pretend *you're* the new manager coming in to lead the group, and take this opportunity to chart a new course of action. I recommend you do this exercise once a year; I used to do it in late December as I was looking ahead to the new year. Similar to Jimmy Stewart's character in the movie *It's a Wonderful Life,* who was given a second chance, you're giving yourself a second chance to lead this group. What are you going to do with that opportunity?

Bootstrap
Takeaways

Write a Letter to Your Successor

1. Use this exercise to recharge your agenda: Where are your key leverage points? What would you do if you were starting in the role today?

2. Put your leadership innovation cap on: What needs shaking up? What needs a new approach?

3. Be bold but realistic. Make meaningful leadership moves, designed to get your team going or challenge them in new ways.

Where Do You Go
From Here?

I HOPE YOU FOUND the ideas in this book useful as you took charge of your own leadership development. How does it feel to be improving your leadership skills? I bet you're getting a lot of positive feedback from your colleagues, which has to feel good. I expect your boss is noticing a difference, too. I'm sure you're feeling more confident with these new leadership behaviors; you're almost certainly better equipped to take on any new challenges that come your way. You're probably enjoying your job more, too. That's great—I'm proud of you. Working on your own game isn't an easy challenge, so you should feel good about the journey to become a better leader. And it's definitely a journey; you're now on a path that never really ends. Self-development takes discipline and dedication, and it's often the first thing we put aside when we get busy or stressed. So don't neglect your development or take it for granted when things heat up around you—keep working to improve your leadership. Resist the temptation to say: *"OK, I applied a few of the techniques this year, I'm good for awhile."* Keep stretching yourself. You've built the development mindset, so remind yourself of how good it feels to be improving your skills.

Speaking of the path, what's around the next bend? How do you keep the momentum going? For starters, pick up this book once a month and read (or reread) a few chapters. Keep searching the book for new ideas or techniques to try out, and talk with your direct reports about how you can continue to apply the lessons you're learning. One thing you might do if you lead a team of managers is take a chapter a week and discuss it as a team; use the book to encourage other leaders in the organization to develop their leadership skills. You've doing a great job of developing your own leadership—now it's time to pay it forward to others.

Second, strive to turn your new behaviors into regular practices. I've found the best way to do this is to "put yourself out there" by telling others what you're working on, and asking for feedback on how you're doing. You've *been* doing it, so I know you can *keep* doing it. Declare your intentions, be transparent about the skills you're trying to improve, and ask others to hold you accountable. That's the best way to ensure that you're cementing new behaviors.

Third, continue to be on the lookout for opportunities to add something new to your leadership toolkit. Be the kind of leader that "sees around corners" and anticipates where the next big move is coming from and then adapt your leadership style accordingly. You can be your own "advance scout" when it comes to leadership development. Look at change as an opportunity to keep your leadership skills ahead of the competition. You're making change work for *you* while reading this book. Keep it up!

Fourth, look above you in the organization. If you truly want to "break out and move up," pay close attention to what's expected of leaders at the next level. How do they get things done? What skills are they leveraging? What behaviors are ingrained in the culture that you still need to adopt? Once you've mastered how to lead at this level, start building a plan to polish or develop the skills you'll need at the next level. Working to improve your leadership style is paying off for you. Guess what? It will continue to do so if you stay in a learning mode and keep making new development plans.

Finally, remind yourself of why you wanted to be a leader in the first place. You got into a leadership role because you like helping other people do extraordinary things. Never lose sight of the fact that leadership is about helping others be successful, or better yet, helping them to achieve their hopes and dreams. You're demonstrating that you enjoy the obligations that go with *being* the leader; remember that one of those responsibilities is being a role model for continuous learning and development.

Where do you go from here? Anywhere you want to, really. Because you're becoming a more mature, well-rounded leader. You're teaching yourself to seek feedback, listen more effectively, and try new things. You're stepping out of your Comfort Zone, and adopting a mentality of servant leadership. More importantly, you're making a difference in other people's lives by becoming a better leader. As it turns out, this journey isn't just for you—it's also for the team. And that's a pretty noble purpose. One that should encourage you to keep pulling yourself up by your own bootstraps!

Figures

FIGURE 1: My Leadership Journey

Leadership Roles	Critical Incidents	Lessons Learned
1992–1995: Johnson & Sons—Supervisor	Promoted to supervise my peers	Being the boss is different People will test you
1995–1998: Acme Company—Manager	My boss wasn't trustworthy Firing Stan in '97	Actions speak louder than words You must set high performance standards
1998–2001: ABLE Co.—Director, Marketing	Getting labeled a micro-manager	Delegate and empower the team
2001–2005: Horizon—VP, Sales	Leading through the merger Driving a new market strategy Arguing with Jim at the offsite	People need a reason to believe Sometimes You have to take risks; hold your temper and know your facts
2005–2007: NTS—SVP, New Products	Taking over the products team	Never stop learning
2007–Present: NTS—EVP, New Products	Getting promoted	Stay humble; take others with you

FIGURE 2: 360° Feedback Action Planning Grid

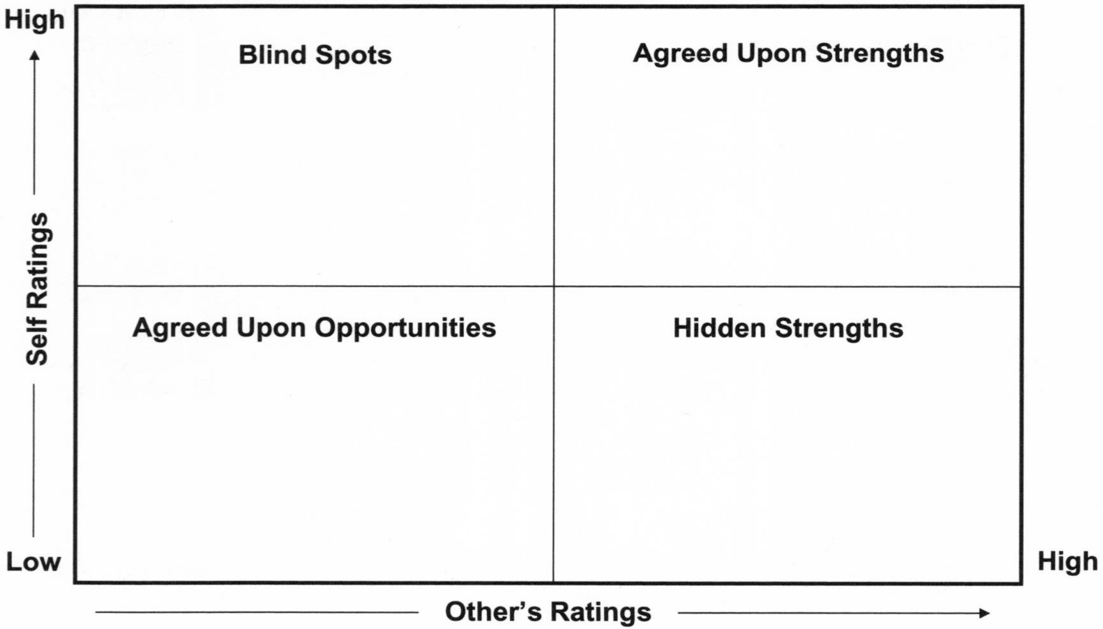

	High
Blind Spots	**Agreed Upon Strengths**
Agreed Upon Opportunities	**Hidden Strengths**

High ← Self Ratings → Low

Other's Ratings → High

FIGURE 3: One-Page Vision, Mission, and Strategy

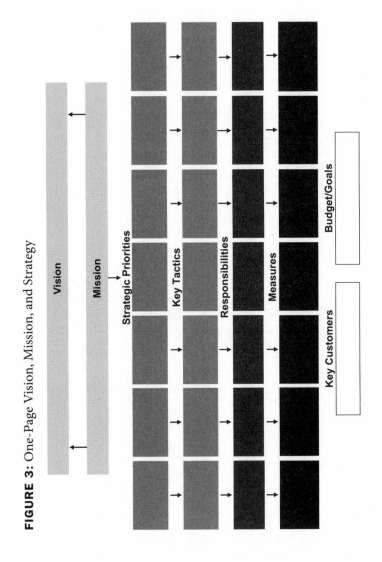

FIGURE 4: Leadership Development Plan

Overall Goal: Be the driving force in making our company the industry leader in organizational development

Developmental Opportunity	Attitude/Mindset/Awareness (noticeable more to me than others)	Visible Behaviors (clearly evident to others)
Increase my visibility and leadership presence	• Continue to seek and be open to feedback on my leadership style • Be organized about how (and when) I spend time with my direct reports—as a group and 1:1	• Engage senior leaders in conversations designed to highlight the team and garner more challenging opportunities for us • Be more visible—spend more time out of the office
Ensure my strategies and results are business-focused	• Focus on being customer relevant—increase my knowledge of what's needed to produce results for our customers • Think strategically—look for opportunities to fit our work into what's going on around us; coach my team on how the pieces fit	• Coach and reward my team for innovation; make innovation a regular topic of conversation in team meetings, and develop a team-wide mindset of the power of innovation • Limit programs to those vital few that will have a significant impact (work on the big things)
Spend more time with my family	• Get better at setting my calendar and creating space for family-only time throughout the week • Focus my attention on how I'm going to spend my time in the evening as I drive home from work	• Leave my Blackberry in my bag when I get home—check it once each night after the kids have gone to bed • Work one hour each weekend day early in the morning, then not for the rest of the day

Key Behavior Enablers

1. *Ask more questions*—be known for the questions I ask, rather than just the answers I give (leverage intellectual curiosity)
2. *Get out of my office*—visit leaders across the company and develop our team's reputation in other parts of the company
3. *Be honest with myself*—be more self-aware; about time spent with the family, what I'm eating, etc.

FIGURE 5: My Leadership Values

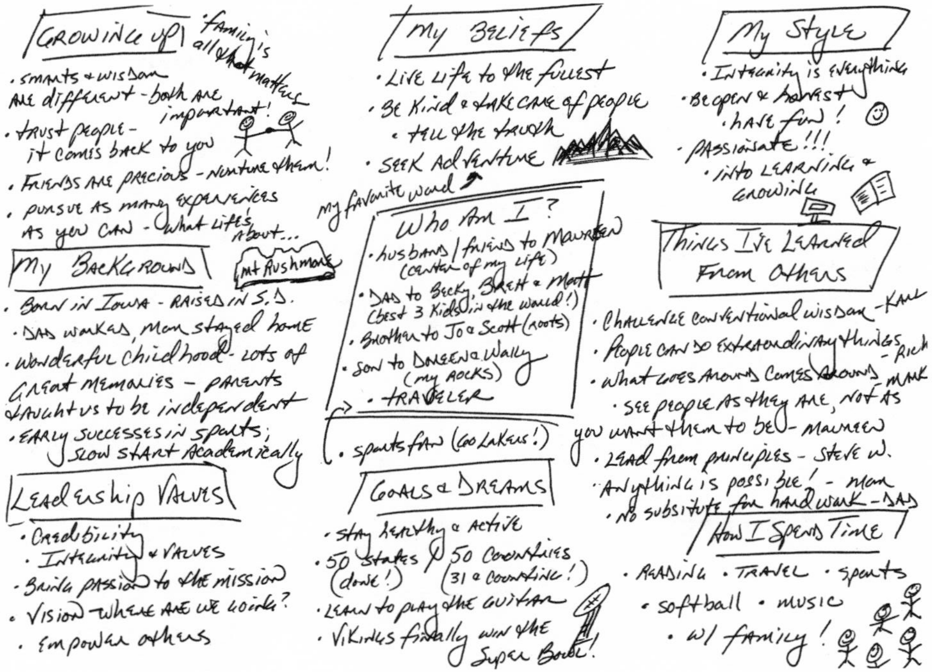

FIGURE 6: Your Comfort Zone

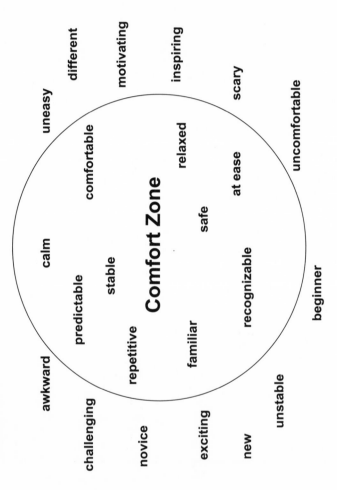

FIGURE 7: Strategy Review Model

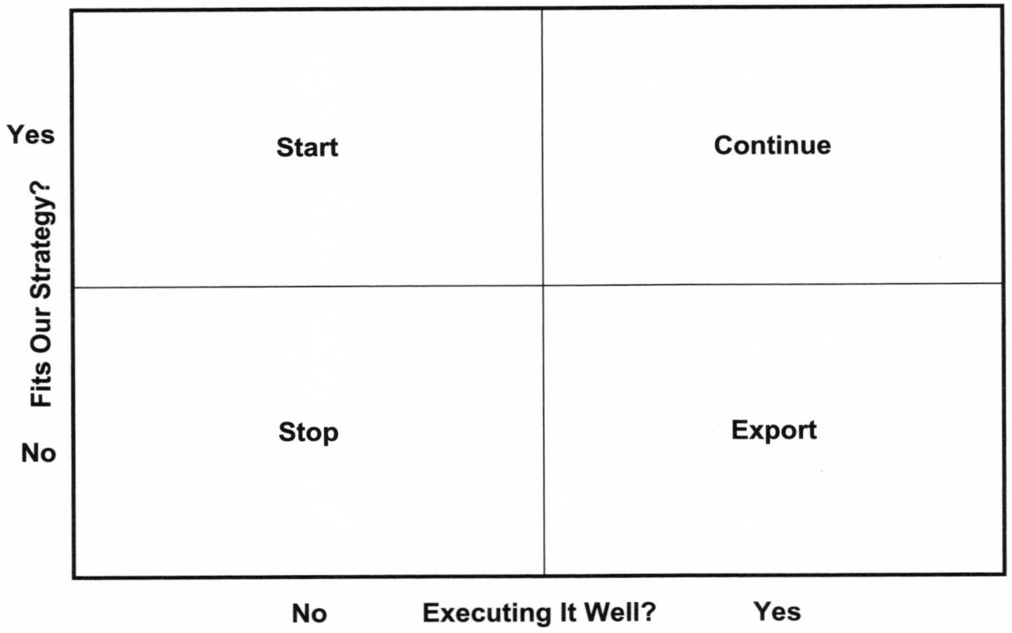

	No	Executing It Well?	Yes
Fits Our Strategy? — Yes	Start		Continue
Fits Our Strategy? — No	Stop		Export

Notes

1. Dave Ulrich, Norm Smallwood, and Kate Sweetman, *The Leadership Code* (Boston: Harvard University Press, 2008).

2. Peter Drucker, "Managing Oneself," *Harvard Business Review* (1999).

3. Bob Eichinger and Michael Lombardo, *The Leadership Machine* (Minneapolis: Lominger Limited, 2001).

4. Tom Peters and Robert Waterman, *In Search of Excellence* (New York: HarperCollins, 1982).

5. Thomas Friedman, *The World Is Flat* (New York: Picador, 2007); Malcolm Gladwell, *The Tipping Point* (Boston: Little, Brown, 2000).

6. John Kotter, Holger Rathgeber, and Spencer Johnson, *Our Iceberg Is Melting* (New York: St. Martins Press, 2006); Patrick Lencioni, *The Five Dysfunctions of a Team* (San Francisco: Jossey-Bass, 2002).

7. Andy Grove, *Only the Paranoid Survive* (New York: Broadway Business, 1999); Lou Gerstner, *Who Says Elephants Can't Dance?* (New York: Harper Paperbacks, 2003); Bill Gates, *The Road Ahead* (Upper Saddle River, NJ: Pearson ESL, 1999); Jack Welch, *Winning* (New York: Harper Business, 2005).

8. Abraham Maslow, "A Theory of Human Motivation," *Psychological Review* (1943).

9. Fritz Heider, *The Psychology of Interpersonal Relations* (New York: John Wiley & Sons, 1958).

10. Frederick Herzberg, *The Motivation to Work* (New York: John Wiley & Sons, 1959.)

11. David McClelland, *The Achieving Society* (New York: Free Press, 1961).

12. Bob Greene, *Once Upon a Town* (New York: Perenniel, 2003).

13. Huston Smith, *The World's Religions* (San Francisco: HarperOne, 2009).

14. Michael Abrashoff, *It's Your Ship* (New York: Business Plus, 2002).

15. Morgan McCall, Michael Lombardo, and Anne Morrison, *The Lessons of Experience* (New York: Free Press, 1988).

16. Nicolaas Pronk et.al, "The Association Between Work Performance and Physical Activity, Cardiorespiratory Fitness and Obesity," *Journal of Occupational and Environmental Medicine* (January, 2004).

17. Jim Loehr and Tony Schwartz, *The Power of Full Engagement* (New York: Free Press, 2004).

18. Noel Tichy, *The Leadership Engine: How Winning Companies Build Leaders at Every Level* (New York: HarperCollins, 2002).

Acknowledgments

FIRST OF ALL, I'd like to thank my wife Maureen, and our three children, Becky, Brett and Matt, for their unwavering support and patience while I wrote this book. You are my greatest source of happiness, and I love you with all my heart. Maureen read and edited many drafts of the book, and because I trust her judgment more than my own, I took every one of her suggestions. Thank you for believing in me and encouraging me along the way, Maureen.

Next, I'd like to thank the many wonderful leaders I've had a chance to work with over the years. You know who you are, and how I feel about you. Thank you for teaching me how to lead with a sense of purpose, fairness, and a relentless pursuit of excellence. In leadership, role models are important, and I had some of the best. I'd also like to thank all of the team members I've had the privilege of leading or working with in my career. The list would be too long to mention everyone by name, and each of them contributed to the leader I am today. Thank you for allowing me to make a few mistakes along the way, and for helping me to improve as a leader. We truly are molded by the people we meet along the journey, and I've been fortunate to work with some terrific colleagues over the years. Thanks for all the great memories.

Without a doubt, this book would not have been possible without the wonderful staff at Berrett-Koehler who bring a personal touch to the business of publishing. I'd like to thank Jeevan Sivasubramaniam for making the entire process work; Dianne Platner, for designing the look and feel of the book; and Deborah

Masi and her team for their expert copyediting. Special thanks to Johanna Vondeling, who saw something in this project from the beginning and gave me countless pieces of advice that always made the book better. Johanna, I don't know where I'd be without your guidance; thank you for believing in me and making this book a reality!

Finally, I'd like to acknowledge my mom and siblings, Scott and Jo, for their support all along the way. Learning to lead effectively starts at home, and I had the foundation of strong family values to build on when it came time to lead others. Mom, you've always been my champion; thanks for supporting me in anything I ever wanted to do.

Index

Index

About the Author

STEVE ARNESON has a passion for leadership and for helping leaders on their journey of exploration and discovery. He believes the best leaders are those that constantly strive to improve—they understand that leading others is a privilege and continuously learn, solicit feedback, and work on their game. This book is about that journey of leadership self-development.

Steve developed his interest in leadership at an early age, playing team sports. He noticed that certain coaches made a difference in his performance; he worked harder for coaches who took a personal interest in him and cared about his development as a player, and he never forgot what it felt like to work for a coach who put the team and his players ahead of his own goals.

As he moved into the workforce, Steve began to experience a different kind of leadership that comes with a relentless pursuit of business results. Steve started to collect examples of leadership that either enabled or derailed a winning team effort. After receiving his doctorate in organizational psychology, he spent the first nine years of his career as a consultant, helping leaders understand their strengths and weaknesses. Steve saw firsthand the power of leading from the heart and how a leader's own passion for continuous improvement often made the difference in how others experienced their leadership.

In 1996, Steve moved to PepsiCo, which has a well-earned reputation for leadership development. Steve continued to work with leaders and soon discovered the power of leveraging a corporate culture that demanded leadership excellence. He also learned how important it is to have senior leaders who are willing to role model a development mindset. Continuing his career as the head of Leadership Development at

America Online and later at Time Warner Cable, Steve began to formulate many of the self-development ideas contained in this book. Through challenging crucibles such as the AOL–Time Warner merger, he helped leaders realize their potential, encouraging managers at all levels to "raise their game" in order to provide their teams with even more effective leadership.

As the head of Executive Talent Management at Capital One, Steve and his team built a number of award-winning leadership programs and were twice named to *Fortune* magazine's "Top 20 Companies for Leaders" list. Steve and his team leveraged a strong culture of learning and development to found Capital One University, which routinely finished in the top twenty-five of *Training* magazine's annual rankings. Throughout his tenure at Capital One, Steve coached and mentored senior leaders, using many of the development techniques outlined in the book.

Steve founded Arneson Leadership Consulting in 2007 and currently works with large and mid-sized companies around the world as an executive coach and as a designer and facilitator of leadership development programs and talent management strategies. Steve brings a practical approach to his work and believes that values-driven leadership is the key ingredient for a successful organization.

Steve speaks regularly on the subjects of leadership and talent management and writes a national leadership column at www.examiner.com. Steve was named one of America's "Top 100 Thought Leaders on Leadership" and one of the country's "Top 25 Leadership Coaches" in 2008–2009 by *Leadership Excellence* magazine. Steve lives with his family in Northern Virginia. You can visit his Web sites at www.arnesonleadership.com or bootstrapleadership.net.

Berrett–Koehler
Publishers

A community dedicated to creating
a world that works for all

Visit Our Website: www.bkconnection.com

Read book excerpts, see author videos and Internet movies, read
our authors' blogs, join discussion groups, download book apps, find
out about the BK Affiliate Network, browse subject-area libraries of
books, get special discounts, and more!

Subscribe to Our Free E-Newsletter, the *BK Communiqué*

Be the first to hear about new publications, special discount offers,
exclusive articles, news about bestsellers, and more! Get on the list
for our free e-newsletter by going to **www.bkconnection.com**.

Get Quantity Discounts

Berrett-Koehler books are available at quantity discounts for orders
of ten or more copies. Please call us toll-free at (800) 929-2929 or
email us at bkp.orders@aidcvt.com.

Join the BK Community

BKcommunity.com is a virtual meeting place where people from
around the world can engage with kindred spirits to create a world
that works for all. **BKcommunity.com** members may create their own
profiles, blog, start and participate in forums and discussion groups,
post photos and videos, answer surveys, announce and register for
upcoming events, and chat with others online in real time. Please join
the conversation!

Mixed Sources

Product group from well-managed
forests, controlled sources and
recycled wood or fiber
www.fsc.org Cert no. SW-COC-003925
© 1996 Forest Stewardship Council

FSC